P9-DHB-944

THE WHAT, WHERE, WHEN OF
THEATER PROPS

An Illustrated Chronology From Arrowheads to Video Games

Other books by Thurston James:

The Theater Props Handbook
The Prop Builder's Molding & Casting Handbook
The Prop Builder's Mask-Making Handbook

THE WHAT, WHERE, WHEN OF
THEATER PROPS

An Illustrated Chronology From Arrowheads to Video Games

THURSTON JAMES

BETTERWAY BOOKS
Cincinnati, Ohio

Cover design by Rick Britton
Illustrations by Thurston James
Typography by Park Lane Associates

The What, Where, When of Theater Props. Copyright © 1992 by Thurston James. Printed and bound in the United States of America. All rights reserved. No part of this book may be reproduced in any form or by any electronic or mechanical means including information storage and retrieval systems without permission in writing from the publisher, except by a reviewer, who may quote brief passages in a review. Published by Betterway Books, an imprint of F&W Publications, Inc., 1507 Dana Avenue, Cincinnati, Ohio 45207. 1-800-289-0963. First edition.

96 96 95 94 93 92   5 4 3 2 1

Library of Congress Cataloging-in-Publication Data

James, Thurston.
    The what, where, when of theater props : an illustrated chronology from arrowheads to video games / Thurston James.
        p.   cm.
    Includes bibliographical references and index.
    ISBN 1-55870-258-X (hardcover) : $27.95. -- ISBN 1-55870-257-1 (pbk.) : $17.95
    1. Stage props--Handbooks, manuals, etc.   I. Title.
PN2091.S8J35 1992
    792'.025--dc20   92-14963
                                                                CIP

ACKNOWLEDGMENTS

Marsha Frank Berke reviewed and critiqued early manuscripts of this book, suggested a format, and gave the book its name. I came to understand and appreciate the terse comments Marsha pencilled in the margin of the text, such as, "Yeah, so?", "Blah blah blah", and "This material belongs in someone else's book."

As the work grew, I occasionally strayed from the agreed-on organizational plan. If I identified a person or defined some procedure I found particularly fascinating, she would nudge me (sometimes gently, sometimes more brusquely), reminding me that we were working on a history of things. Thank you, Marsha.

Contents

Introduction

I've just retired after thirty years in educational theater. I've been a shop carpenter, scenic artist, lighting designer, and technical director, I've taught stagecraft and most recently spent fourteen years as properties master for the UCLA Department of Theater. I've also been a freelance property builder for movies and television. I can tell you, good research material is essential.

I have long believed that every practitioner in "the Business" needs to collect a personal file of clippings and articles of special interest to his craft. The actor might collect character studies— facial features and the body language of youth and old age. A lighting designer might collect an idea file of seasons, sunsets, and storms—noting the effect that these can have on ambient light. The properties master will have the largest file, for it must include *everything*. My file consists of pictures, articles, clippings, and handwritten information collected on specific problems that my prop room came up against while I was there. This research is housed in two tightly packed file cabinets.

You simply cannot be expected to be knowledgeable about objects that were common eight or five or a hundred years ago. For instance, would it be out of period for a Shakespearean character to wear eyeglasses? Could Mercutio, close friend to Romeo, smoke a tobacco pipe? Might Abraham Lincoln as a child have studied his lessons by the light of a kerosene lamp?

Most people have trouble recalling events that happened in their own lifetimes. Can you remember (within five years) when flippers were added to pinball machines, or when Pac-man was introduced as a video game, or when the microwave was generally available for use in the kitchen? How about CD players —when were they first put on the market? Remember the format controversy between Beta and VHS? Early '70s? Middle '80s?

These are more than just trivia questions when a writer or a director is developing a script for production, or for a properties master after the script has been finalized. You may get some of the answers from your own life experience, tying the object to an important event in your past and coming up with the right answer. But if you don't remember, the facts may be tough to pin down. Current history is not easier than ancient history to find in the library.

I hope this book will tell you some of what you need to know. I am sorry, I cannot guarantee all parts and labor: life is too big a machine.

The *What, When, Where* was begun as an attempt put into the hands of theater and movie people a research handbook describing and picturing a wide variety of obscure to pretty common items and placing them in a historical context. I think that I have stayed true to my original intent, even though as the work developed, it became apparent that the contents might be of interest to others outside those fields.

The items are arranged alphabetically within a general subject framework and are also listed in the index. Entries wherever possible include a description and an illustration of an object, its size or dimensions, and the place and time of its introduction into use.

Beyond using the handbook as an illustrated dictionary, and perhaps equally important, try using it to open up new ideas, possibilities that you might not have been aware of for propping a show or film, or for bits of business, by browsing through the pages of any of the subject headings.

There are some admitted holes in the information presented in this book. Research available to us in the West naturally concentrates on the evolution of things here. So did I. The Middle East and the Orient are only mentioned insofar as they are responsible for introducing a new product or invention, and no details are presented regarding an article's development in these regions. It is also possible that there is an unwarranted emphasis on England's importance. A number of the books I used for research were written and proudly published there.

So. Given that, practically speaking, my book could not include details on everything, I decided I would begin the work on a personal level, concentrating on objects that have given me trouble in their time. Counting the major and minor productions, the Department of Theater at UCLA prepares more than fifty different plays in a single year that are performed for a public audience. The prop room supplies the props for all these productions, and we are involved in designing and building properties for about half of them. I've had my troubles. Much of the information I pulled from my own files was too specific for general use, being addressed to the needs of a particular director or a certain designer's approach to a production. I was, however, able to produce a roll call of topics which evolved into the current Table of Contents. I went to my own library and then to the public library, expanding the research until—as I now believe—it can be valuable to all those people who work at entertaining us and making us think and see in new ways.

Thurston James
January 1992

PART I: DAILY LIVING

Eating
Drinking
Smoking Pipes
Games
Furniture
Clocks and Watches
Lamps and Lanterns
Matches
Writing Tools and Supplies
Eyeglasses
Hearing Aids
Appliances

Eating

FOODS

Man has eaten foods from the "four basic food groups" for as long as we have recorded history. Butter and bread, not found in a natural state, came last. Early breads were a fried mixture of grain and oil, much like the flour tortilla or pita bread we see today. Butter was made by violently shaking a goatskin filled with milk. But even these foods were manufactured from antiquity.

A man of any society can only eat the things available to him, and not everything is available worldwide. For hundreds of years people of the Orient lived mostly on rice; the Indians of Panama ate fruits and vegetables; and the Alaskan Eskimo's primary diet consisted of meat and fish.

All eating was done with the fingers (or fingers and a knife) from prehistory into colonial times. (See Utensils.)

The following inventory places many food items and food-producing companies in their proper time frames. The list is organized chronologically. An item with multiple entries is placed according to the earliest date.

Brief History of Food		
BREAD	fried grain and oil mixtures are used worldwide	antiquity
	leavened bread is baked in an oven	2500 B.C.
PRESERVING FOODS	drying fruits and meat is practiced	antiquity
	smoking meat is practiced	antiquity
	Romans pack foods in imported ice	200 B.C.
	canning foods in sealed jars is introduced in France	1810
	railroad car is refrigerated with ice for shipping food	early 1800s
	commercial refrigerator is invented for cold storage	late 1800s
SUGAR	is probably first cultivated in India	antiquity
SAUSAGE	intestine skin stuffed with spiced meat is made in Babylonia	3000 B.C.
KETCHUP	a sauce of vinegar, spice, and anchovies is made in Rome	300 A.D.
	a sauce made from tomato puree is developed	1790
	Heinz tomato ketchup is marketed	1876

PRETZEL	is invented by an Italian monk and given to children as a reward	610 A.D.
PASTA	native to China as noodles, is brought to Italy by Marco Polo	1200s
	put in jars and first marketed in America by Chef Boy-ar-dee	1920
HAMBURGER	low-grade beef is ground and spiced in Hamburg, Germany	1200s
	hamburger steak is brought to America	1800s
	a small ground steak is served on a bun at the World's Fair	1904
DOUGHNUT	sweetened biscuit dough is deep-fried in Holland	1500s
	a hole is cut in the center	mid-1800s
ICE CREAM	is invented in Italy	1500s
	first ice cream factory in America is operating in Baltimore	1851
	the ice cream sundae is first made	1890
	the ice cream cone is developed for the World's Fair	1904
	Eskimo Pie, a chocolate-coated ice cream bar, is introduced	1922
POTATO	native to South America, is introduced to Europe	1500s
CHOCOLATE	native to Central America, is introduced to Spain	mid-1500s
	chocolate candy bar—first produced in Switzerland	1819
PANCAKE	cornmeal pancakes are made in Colonial America	1600s
	Aunt Jemima pancake mix is marketed	1889
POPCORN	native to America, is introduced to England	1600s
COFFEE	native to Arabia, is introduced to Italy	mid-1600s
	Postum instant coffee is developed	1929
	Nescafe instant coffee is marketed by Nestlé	1937
CROISSANT	is first made in Vienna to commemorate a victory over the Turks	1683
TOMATO	is not appreciated as a food until	late 1700s
SANDWICH	is invented in England as a quick snack	1762
PEANUTS	not appreciated as a food for people until	1800s
	P.T. Barnum sells small packages at his circus	1880
	Planters markets roasted and salted peanuts	1906
	peanut butter is associated with jelly	1920s
COOKIES	Graham cracker is marketed as a health food	1830s
	Fig Newton — a stuffed cookie containing fig jam is marketed	1895
	Animal Crackers are made by Nabisco	1902
	Oreo is one of the first cookies marketed by Nabisco	1912
	chocolate chip cookie is first made at Toll House Inn, Massachusetts	1930
FRANKFURTER	this mild sausage has its beginnings in Germany	1850
	Hot dog, a name for the frankfurter, is coined by an American cartoonist	1906
POTATO CHIP	deep-fried potato slices are introduced in New York	1853
CHEWING GUM	flavorings are added to chicle to make chewing gum	1860s
	Wrigley's Spearmint and Juicy Fruit are marketed	1892
	Chiclets introduces candy-coated gum	1910
	Bubble gum is developed and marketed by Fleers	1928
FROZEN FOOD	the first commercial frozen food is prepared	1865
	Clarence Birdseye develops the quick-freezing process	1925
VANILLA	artificial flavor is formulated to simulate real vanilla	1874
COCA-COLA	"Coke" formula is invented and mixed with soda water	1886
	familiar Coke bottle is designed	1913
	"New Coke" is introduced	1985
	"Classic Coke" is reinstated two months later	1985

BREAKFAST CEREAL	Corn Flakes is marketed by Kelloggs	1890s
	Shredded Wheat is developed by Ralston Purina	1890s
	Oatmeal is marketed by Quaker Oats	1901
CRACKER JACKS	mixture of candied popcorn and peanuts is packaged and sold	1893

UTENSILS

For thousands of years civilized man, even in polite society, ate with his fingers. A few rules were established along the way, such as using only three fingers — the thumb, forefinger, and middle finger—but accepted custom said "pick up the food and eat it."

ELECTRIC KNIFE The electric knife with a serrated cutting edge and replaceable blades was first marketed in the early 1960s and is widely used for carving the Thanksgiving turkey.

FORK The fork had a terrible time finding acceptance at the dining table. The first fork was introduced in Tuscany, Italy in 1000 A.D. (about the same time spaghetti was introduced by Marco Polo—could there be a connection?). This fork had two tines, and during its experimental period it was belittled in foreign courts as being no better than a knife and a bit "show-offy."

Finally, in the 18th century, eating with the fingers was declared gauche, and the four-tined fork became a sign of luxury, refinement, and status.

KNIFE The first utensil was the knife. In 1000 B.C., the same knife that killed and cleaned the hunt could be used to pierce a bite-sized piece of cooked meat and carry it to the hunter's mouth.

A knife used specifically for dining did not appear till the 14th century. Actually, a pair of knives was used, one for holding the meat, the other to cut a chunk from the portion, spear it, and deliver it.

SPOON Most liquids runny enough to be served in a bowl were sipped directly from the bowl. The spoon was used for thicker stews and porridge. Spoons were made in 1000 B.C. from hollowed bone, horn, or sea shells. The wealthy classes of Greece and Rome used spoons of bronze and silver. For hundreds of years, when the fingers proved ineffective, a wooden spoon was the accepted alternative.

Drinking

―――――― **FERMENTED BEVERAGES** ――――――

Any drinkable liquid containing sugar and yeast can be made into an alcoholic beverage by allowing it to ferment. Our ancestors made fermented beverages from honey, dates, milk, molasses, palms, peppers, and pomegranates. The popular fermented drinks in the United States today are beer and wine. Alcoholic beverages are often made stronger by putting them through a distillation process. These are called spirits.

ALE A fermented malt drink resembling beer, but having more body.

PLACE: England and Ireland

TIME: Initially produced in 1400s

BEER Any undistilled fermented malt beverage. Early beers made of fermented milk or the juice of a local plant were produced in many countries. The beer we know, made of fermented grains, was developed in Northern Europe.

PLACE: Germany, Bohemia, and Denmark

TIME: Introduced and developed from 1300 to 1400

BITTERS A liquor flavored with bitter herbs, roots, bark, or fruit.

BOURBON A whiskey made from corn. Bourbon was first produced by a resident of Kentucky, Elijah Craig.

PLACE: Bourbon County, Kentucky

TIME: 1789

BRANDY An alcoholic beverage made by distilling wine. The finest brandy comes from France and is called cognac. Fruit brandies are made with apples, apricots, blackberries, pineapple, or other fruits.

COGNAC A brandy distilled from wines produced near Cognac, France. In a less strict sense, cognac can refer to any brandy.

CORDIAL See Liqueur.

GIN A liquor made from rye and flavored with juniper berries. Gin was first produced by a Dutch physician, Doctor Sylvius.

PLACE: Holland

TIME: Developed in 1600s

LIQUEUR A strong alcoholic liquor flavored with herbs, spices, flowers, fruits, and sugar. Some are fortified with additional alcohol. (Also "cordial.")

PLACE: France

TIME: Introduced in 1500s

LIQUOR   Any alcoholic beverage, especially one made of distilled spirits.

RUM   A liquor prepared by distilling a fermented mixture of molasses or sugar cane.

PLACE: Caribbean

TIME: Introduced in 1500s

RYE   A whiskey made from the grain of the rye plant. The brewing process is identical to that used in producing bourbon, only the grain is different.

SCOTCH   A whiskey originally made in Scotland. Scotch is a blend of malt whiskey and other high-proof grain whiskeys.

TEQUILA   A liquor distilled from the juice of the stem of the agave or century plant. Popular in Mexico.

VODKA   A liquor made by distilling a fermented mash of cereal grains or potatoes. In the early 1800s, a process of charcoal filtering was discovered, which removed a flavor that many people considered objectionable. The tasteless, colorless vodka became popular worldwide.

PLACE: Russia and Poland

TIME: Introduced in 1300s

WHISKEY   A liquor made by distilling a solution of fermented grains, usually wheat, malted barley, rye, or corn.

WINE   An alcoholic beverage made from fermented grapes or berries.

―――――――――――――― COCKTAILS OF THE PAST ――――――――――――

A cocktail is a drink consisting of two or more ingredients, one of which is alcoholic. The first mixed drink likely occurred as soon as wine was discovered and mixed with water.

CAUDLE   A warm gruel made of ground corn meal, wine or ale, sugar, and spices. Caudle was intended to be easily digested and was served to invalids.

PLACE: Europe

TIME: 1300s to 1600s

LAMB'S WOOL   Ale mixed with apple pulp, sugar, and nutmeg. The apple pulp floated on the surface of the liquid and was reminiscent of wool.

PLACE: Europe

TIME: 1300s to 1600s

MULLED ALE   A sweetened ale drink, spiced with ginger and served hot.

PLACE: Europe

TIME: 1300s to 1600s

POSSET   A hot drink made of milk curdled with spiced ale or wine.

PLACE: England

TIME: 1600s

TODDY   A hot drink made with whiskey, water, sugar, and spices. The toddy was an accepted 18th century cold remedy.

PLACE: England and United States

TIME: 1700s

WASSAIL   A Christmas punch consisting of sweetened wine flavored with nutmeg, cinnamon, cloves, and apple.

PLACE: England

TIME: 1100s

BEER GLASSES

Bartenders tell us that size, thickness, and shape of a beer glass are very important, having a significant effect on both the temperature of the beer and the amount of head produced.

PITCHER
54-64 OZ.

SCHOONER
12-14 OZ.

MUG/
STEIN
10-12 OZ.

TANKARD
10-12 OZ.

HOUR GLASS
8-10 OZ.

SHELL
8-12 OZ.

PILSNER
10-12 OZ.

FOOTED PILSNER
10-12 OZ.

WINE GLASSES

Vintage Wine Glasses Fine quality lead oxide wine goblets, demonstrating the craftsman's pride in his product, were made in the 17th century. Glass drinking cups of this period had definite identifying characteristics and were known by their distinctive design features, such as drawn stem, air twist stem, waisted bowl, and dome foot.

PLACE: Produced in Europe, particularly England and Venice

TIME: 1600s

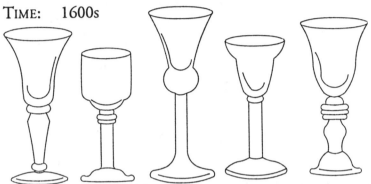

The Modern Wine Glass Today's wine drinker uses wine glasses designed to add to the enjoyment of his drink through the senses of sight and smell. Most wine glasses are made to be crystal clear so the color of the wine can be seen. The traditional foot-and-stem is retained on modern glasses not only because the shape is pleasing, but also because it allows the light to enter the bowl of the glass from every direction and the drinker to handle the glass without warming its contents. The mouth of the glass is made slightly smaller than the body in order to hold the aroma.

Some wines are traditionally associated with particular shapes of glasses and, when the occasion supports it, there may be good reason to serve a wine in its traditional glass. It is likely, however, that only an expert would be aware if a burgundy was served in a bordeaux-style glass, and even then, he would not be offended. Either the bordeaux or the burgundy glass could be used for most red or white wines.

BORDEAUX BURGUNDY HOCK ALSACE SAUCER CHAMPAGNE TULIP CHAMPAGNE FLUTE CHAMPAGNE

COCKTAIL GLASSES

Modern Cocktail Glasses With the ingredients available today, the number of possible cocktails seems to be unlimited, and new variations are being invented all the time. Occasionally a distillery will concoct a recipe that shows signs of being particularly promising and use a glass with a distinct shape to help merchandise the new drink. If the drink truly becomes popular, the glass may acquire a new name. There are currently some 15 to 18 different styles of glasses used to serve cocktails.

BRANDY SNIFTER A stemmed glass used for serving liqueur and brandy. The glass is never filled. The drink lies in the lower portion of the glass and the aroma fills the bowl.

SIZE: 6 ounces

COCKTAIL GLASS A stemmed glass used for serving the many drinks that are made by blending liqueur with cream, and for a few other specific cocktails, such as Bacardi cocktails, daiquiris, and martinis.

SIZE: 4 to 6 ounces

COLLINS GLASS A tumbler with vertical sides, for drinks that are mixed with any of a variety of liquors, lemon juice, and carbonated water. The Tom Collins, made with gin, is strongly associated with this glass.

SIZE: 10 to 12 ounces

COOLER A tumbler used for tall mixed drinks of the Collins and fizz variety. This glass is also used for wine coolers made by mixing wine with soda water or lemon-flavored sodas.

SIZE: 16 ounces

CORDIAL A small stemmed glass for serving cordials (or liqueurs) straight from the bottle.

SIZE: 1 to 2 ounces

COUPETTE A larger stemmed glass for serving double-size sour drinks (those with no soda). The margarita is firmly associated with this style of glass.

SIZE: 6 to 8 ounces

FOOTED GLASS A glass that is designed for the bowl to rest on a very short stemmed foot.

HIGHBALL GLASS A utility tumbler for serving most drinks made from liquor and a non-alcoholic mix. The highball glass can be used to serve a gin and tonic, bloody mary, or screwdriver, the original highball (whiskey and ginger ale), and many others. The Collins glass is a specialized highball glass specifically for drinks made with liquor and sweetened lemon juice.

SIZE: 8 to 10 ounces

HURRICANE   A glass designed in the shape of a hurricane lamp chimney. The hurricane glass is used to serve specialty tropical fruit drinks.

SIZE: 10 to 16 ounces

JIGGER   A tumbler for measuring liquors as they are being mixed. A shot glass is a jigger that is used for serving and consuming undiluted liquor.

SIZE: 1 to 3 ounces

LIQUEUR   A footed glass for serving sipping liqueurs. (See Cordial.)

SIZE: 1 to 2 ounces

MARGARITA GLASS   A stemmed glass, the coupette, has been associated with the margarita since its invention. Served with a salted rim.

MARTINI GLASS   A stemmed cocktail glass with straight sides has come to be associated with the martini.

SIZE: 5 ounces

OLD-FASHIONED GLASS   A certain rocks glass with straight sides has been used for a very long time to serve a drink called an old-fashioned. This drink is made by mixing bourbon and soda and serving over ice.

SIZE: 6 ounces

ROCKS GLASS   A tumbler used to serve a variety of two-liquor drinks over ice cubes. These drinks are made with a base liquor (scotch, vodka, brandy), a sweet liqueur (kahlua, amaretto, creme de menthe), and ice. Recently some rocks glasses have been made with a short stemmed foot.

SIZE: 6 to 12 ounces

SHOT GLASS   A glass used to measure and serve liquor straight from the bottle.

SIZE: 1 to 3 ounces

SOUR GLASS   A stemmed glass for the smaller sour drinks containing liquor and lemon juice with no soda water. The whiskey sour has come to be associated with this glass.

SIZE: 4½ ounces

SNIFTER   A footed glass usually a good deal larger than the 2 ounces of liqueur it is intended to hold. The aroma of the drink collects in the bowl and adds to the flavor experience.

SIZE: 6 ounces

STEMMED GLASS   A glass designed to have a bowl, a foot, and a stem.

TUMBLER   A style of glass having a flat bottom with no foot or stem.

ZOMBIE GLASS A tall Collins glass. The glass is not used exclusively for the zombie, but it is associated with the invention of this drink made of various rums, liqueur, and fruit juice.

SIZE: 12 ounces

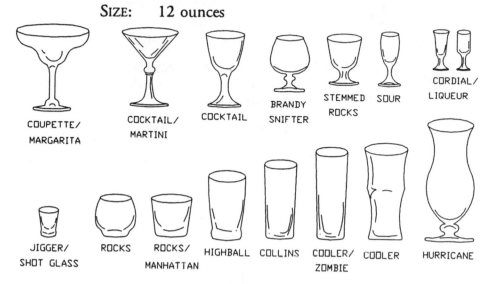

GARNISHES

Only a few drinks are served with a garnish. A well-equipped home bar includes quartered limes, sliced oranges and lemons, maraschino cherries, olives, and perhaps cocktail onions. There are a few more exotic garnishes you may want to stock, but only when the need arises.

Drink —	Garnish
Bloody Mary	Celery stalk
Gibson	Onion
Gin and Tonic	Lime section
Manhattan	Cherry
Martini	Olive
Mint Julep	Mint sprig
Pina Colada	Pineapple slice
Old Fashioned	Cherry
Sours (most)	Cherry
Tom Collins	Cherry
Tropical drinks	Orange slice
Whisky Sour	Cherry
Vodka Gimlet	Lime section

CUPS, POTS, AND URNS

Pottery and wooden vessels have been in continual use from prehistoric times. The Bronze Age came to Europe in about 1800 B.C. and, for the first time, pots and cups were made of metal. Crude glass vessels were produced from 1500 B.C. Glass blowing was introduced in about 30 B.C., and glassware became inexpensive and popular.

In a parallel development, containers for liquids were made from raw hide and leather. From the earliest times, animal skins were cut and sewn so one leg would form a pouring spout; they were used for wine or water. Sealed leather vessels were introduced in the mid-1300s, and remained popular in medieval taverns even after pewter flagons were introduced because they were less expensive and much lighter.

All along the way, excellent examples of fine craftsmanship can be found that stand out from the utilitarian. Fine porcelain vases were uncovered at Tutankhamen's tomb. The Greeks and Romans produced exquisitely carved and decorated silverwork. The 10th century church, needing several different ceremonial vessels, commissioned some of the finest gold cups and bowls and silver pitchers ever made.

ALEYARD A drinking glass and liquid measure. It is very narrow, and a yard long. The aleyard holds about one quart of liquid.

SIZE: 3 feet long

PLACE: Italy and Germany

TIME: 1500s

AMPHORA A two-handled earthenware jar for storing or shipping grain, honey, oil, or wine. This design is characterized by a tapering egg-shaped body, often with a rounded or pointed base. Amphoras are transported by loosely tying two together and slinging them over a donkey's back or, depending on the weight, carrying them over the shoulders of a man.

The round base does not permit the vessel to stand on a flat surface, but it can be pressed into loose sand and supported by piling additional sand around the base. The amphora became a standard for measuring a quantity of fluid. In Greece the fluid unit was about 10 gallons; in Rome the unit was about 6½ gallons.

SIZE: 2½ to 3 feet tall

PLACE: Greece and Rome

TIME: 500 B.C. to 400 A.D.

AMPULLA A glass or pottery container used by the ancient Romans to hold ointment or perfume. It is also used by the church to hold water for the Eucharist, or to hold oil in performing ceremonies, especially the crowning of kings.

SIZE: 4 inches tall

PLACE AND TIME: Rome - 200 B.C.

Europe - 300 to 1200 A.D.

BARREL A cylindrical vessel made of wooden staves and bound by hoops. The barrel holds 31.5 U.S. gallons of liquid (or 36 imperial gallons). (See chart for comparing Vessel Volumes.)

BATH A pot holding about 6 gallons of liquid. This Hebrew word means "daughter" and designates a large jug that might be used to carry home a one-day supply of domestic water from the local well.

BLACK JACK A leather vessel for serving beer. The seams in the leather are hand-sewn and sealed with tar or wax to make them liquid-tight.

SIZE: 9 inches tall

PLACE: Europe (taverns)

TIME: 1300 to 1700

BOMBARD A leather vessel with hand-sewn seams for carrying beer. The leather bombard was a popular pitcher in medieval taverns for over 400 years.

SIZE: 1 foot tall

PLACE: Europe (taverns)

TIME: 1300 to 1700

BOTTEL A leather vessel for storing wine or water. It was made by folding a large piece of leather onto itself and stitching a wide seam on each side. The top had a narrow opening for pouring and was cut with a pair of slots for a strap handle.

SIZE: 1 foot tall

PLACE: Europe (taverns)

TIME: 1300 to 1700

CANTHARUS A wide-mouthed drinking bowl standing on a short stemmed foot, with two handles that rise above the brim. The cantharus was used at the banquets of the ancient Greeks.

SIZE: 8 inches tall

PLACE: Greece

TIME: 500 B.C.

CASK A general term used to describe barrels used for holding liquids.

The term may also refer to the liquid that a specific cask may hold.

CAUDLE CUP A cup with two large handles for serving caudle, a spiced gruel mixed with wine, to a sick person.

SIZE: 4 inches tall

PLACE: Europe, particularly England

TIME: Early 1600s

CISTERN In ancient times, a chest or box. In modern times it is a large receptacle for water, especially for collecting rainwater. In distilleries, the cistern is a large tank for storing beer.

CRUCIBLE A vessel or pot that is baked or tempered to resist extreme heat. It is used for melting metals or certain minerals.

SIZE: 3 inches high - apothecary

3 feet high - foundry

CRUET A small glass-stoppered bottle for oil or vinegar. The cruet is also used to serve wine or water in the celebration of the Eucharist.

SIZE: 5 inches tall

TIME: 1000 A.D.

DECANTER A long-necked bottle used to pour the liquor from its sediment. A decanter is also a stoppered bottle for serving wine. The drawing shows a modern decanter. It is frequently decorative, made of cut glass, holding about a liter of liquor.

SIZE: 8 inches tall

DRINKING HORN A cattle horn used for drinking. The horn was cut, hollowed, cleaned, and embellished with carvings, metal bands, and sometimes feet. The Saxons learned of drinking horns from the Romans.

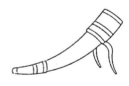

Sizes varied. Early Saxon horns were as long as 2 feet and held nearly a gallon. (See also Rhyton.)

SIZE: The horn in the drawing is 6 inches high when standing on a table.

PLACE AND TIME: Rome - 100 A.D.

Germany and England (Saxons) - 300 A.D.

Scandinavia (Nords) - 800 A.D.

EWER A wide-spouted jug or pitcher for holding and pouring water for washing. The ewer was used continuously from the Roman period to the time indoor plumbing became common. It was usually found in the presence of a basin and towel on a wash-stand.

SIZE: 14 inches tall

PLACE: Europe and United States

TIME: 100 A.D. to late 1800s

FIRKIN A small cask for beer, butter, fish, soap, etc., equal to ¼ barrel. Since barrel sizes varied, it is difficult to pin down the exact dry measure of a cask. The firkin is, however, much more exact in its liquid measure. It is equivalent to 9 imperial gallons or 7.5 U.S. gallons. (See chart for a comparison of Vessel Volumes.)

FLAGON A vessel used to serve wine or beer. It has a handle, a narrow neck, a spout, and a lid—often hinged. The flagon is also used as an approximate unit of measure—equal to the amount of liquid that such a vessel can hold.

SIZE: 10 inches tall

PLACE: Germany

TIME: 1600s

GOBLET A drinking cup with a base and a stand but no handles.

SIZE: 6 inches tall

PLACE: Rome, Greece, Europe

TIME: 1000 B.C. to 1800s A.D.

GODET A pewter tankard (see Tankard).

TIME: 1300s

HIN A Hebrew water pot that holds about 1 U.S. gallon. The hin is ¹/₆ of a bath (see Bath).

HANAP A pewter goblet used in taverns. The hanap has a base, a stem, and sometimes a cover. Like the goblet, this cup can have a very simple design or it can be crafted in precious metals with ornate decorations. When the cover is in place it may resemble an acorn.

PLACE: England

TIME: 1300s

HOGSHEAD A large cask holding from 63 to 140 U.S. gallons. For liquid measure specifically, it means 63 gallons. (See chart for a comparison of Vessel Volumes.)

HOMER A dry measure equal to what a donkey might be expected to carry—about 6¼ bushels.

HORN FLAGON A flagon made from the end of a large diameter horn. It is decorated and made watertight with silver work.

SIZE: 10 inches tall

PLACE: Europe

TIME: 900 to 1600

HYDRIA   A pitcher with three handles and a large, roomy body for storing water or wine.

SIZE: 2 feet tall

PLACE: Greece

TIME: 800 B.C.

IMPERIAL GALLON   A British unit of measure. The imperial gallon is equal to 277.42 cubic inches or about 1⅕ U.S. gallons.

JORUM   A pewter drinking bowl for serving beer in taverns or inns. The jorum holds about ½ pint; the word sometimes refers to this measure of liquid.

KEG   A small strong barrel usually holding 5 to 10 gallons, or 100 pounds when used for nails. (See chart for a comparison of Vessel Volumes.)

KRATER   A vase-shaped pitcher for mixing water and wine.

SIZE: 2½ feet tall

PLACE: Greece and Rome

TIME: 500 B.C. to 300 A.D.

KYLIX   A shallow earthenware drinking cup with a foot, stem, and two small handles. The kylix was used chiefly at banquets.

SIZE: 4 inches tall

PLACE: Greece and Rome

TIME: 500 B.C. to 300 A.D.

LOVING CUP   A large drinking cup with two or more handles. The cup is passed from guest to guest at festive occasions.

SIZE: 7 inches tall, 6 inches in diameter

PLACE: Originally introduced in Europe

TIME: Late 1700s to the present

MAZER   A simple wooden drinking bowl. The medieval mazer was made of maple and shaped like a bird's nest. The better bowls were trimmed in gold or silver. In later years, the mazer was crafted completely of metal.

SIZE: 3 inches tall

PLACE: Europe

TIME: 1000s

MULLER A cone-shaped container made of tin for warming ale. The muller is filled with a serving of spiced ale and inserted into a bed of hot coals, quickly heating it. The drink is then poured and served piping hot in a mug or tankard.

SIZE: 9 inches tall

PLACE: England, Ireland, and Scotland

TIME: 1700s

NOGGIN A small mug, originally made of wood. Later, it referred to any similar mug, regardless of the material from which it was made. The noggin is also a measure for ale, equal to about ¼ pint.

SIZE: 2 inches tall

PLACE: Ireland

TIME: 1300s

OINOCHOE A pitcher or vase with a handle. The oinochoe was used in ancient Greece to transfer wine from the krater to the goblet or the kylix for drinking. (See Krater, Goblet, and Kylix.)

SIZE: 12 to 15 inches tall

PLACE: Greece

TIME: 800 B.C.

PATERA A sacrificial plate as deep as a shallow saucer, made of metal or pottery, and having two handles. It was used for liquid offerings.

SIZE: 3 inches tall

PLACE: Rome

TIME: 500 B.C.

PIGGIN An earthenware or wooden dipper. The piggin holds nearly a quart and is sometimes used as a drinking cup for beer, ale, or cider.

SIZE: 4 inches tall

PLACE: Europe, particularly England

TIME: 1500s

POCULUM A footed and stemmed drinking cup having no handles.

PHIAL A broad, shallow drinking vessel. (See also Vial.)

RHYTON A drinking cup, originally made in Greece of a ram's horn. The rhyton is frequently made of pottery or metal, having a base designed to resemble the head of a woman, an animal, or a mythological beast. (See also Drinking Horn.)

SIZE: 8 inches tall

PLACE AND TIME: Rome - 100 A.D.

Germany (Saxons) - 300 A.D.

Scandinavia (Nords) - 800 A.D.

STANDING CUP Any drinking cup that does not rest on its own base but depends on a stem and foot for support. (See Goblet.)

STOUP A drinking mug or tankard. The stoup is also a measure; such a mug will hold about a pint.

SIZE: 8 inches tall

PLACE: Europe, especially Germany

TIME: 1500 to 1600

STIRRUP CUP A farewell drink served to a rider after he has mounted his horse and is ready to depart.

PLACE: England, Ireland, Scotland

TIME: Late 1700s

TANKARD A large beer mug or other drinking vessel with a handle. The tankard often has a hinged lid.

SIZE: 6 to 9 inches tall

PLACE: Europe, especially Germany

TIME: 1500 to 1800

TAPPET-HEN A huge pewter flagon containing 3 quarts.

SIZE: 1 foot tall

PLACE: Scotland

TIME: 1600s

TAZZA A bowl-shaped wine cup on a stem and foot. It resembles the modern day champagne glass. The tazza is usually made of silver and is ornamented with patterns and frequently with inscriptions.

SIZE: 5 inches tall

PLACE: Rome

TIME: 100 A.D.

TOBY JUG A small pottery pitcher or mug in the form of a stout man wearing a three-cornered hat. The corner on Toby's hat forms a spout for pouring or drinking.

SIZE: 7 inches tall

PLACE: England

TIME: 1700s

TUB A round, broad wooden container, usually formed with staves and hoops, a flat bottom, and handles on the sides. The tub is essentially half of a barrel. The term also covers a liquid measure equal to about 4 gallons.

TUMBLER A drinking vessel made of glass. This early glass cup ends in a round ball of glass and, although it is bottom-heavy, it is likely to rock and tumble over when it is set down. If the drink cannot be downed in one swallow, the glass must be held in the hand.

SIZE: 5 inches tall

PLACE: Europe

TIME: Mid-1600s

URN A vase or jar, usually with a foot or pedestal and lid. The urn is variously used as a water pot or for holding the ashes of the dead after cremation. In ancient Rome, the urn was used as a liquid measure containing about 3½ gallons.

SIZE: 1 foot to 1½ feet tall

PLACE: Worldwide

TIME: Very ancient origin

VASE Any open-mouthed container, made of pottery, glass, metal, etc., and used for decoration or to display flowers.

TIME: Ancient origin to the present

VAT A large cask for storing liquids while they ferment or ripen. The vat can also be an open tank or tub for soaking fabric in a dyeing process or for holding leather in a tanning process. In

Belgium and the Netherlands the vat is equal to a hectoliter (about 26.4 gallons).

VIAL A small bottle usually of glass for containing medicines or other liquids.

WATER BOTTLE A container variously made of animal skin, glass, rubber, etc., to carry and store water.

Vessel Volumes

CONTAINER	IMPERIAL GALLONS	BARRELS	HOGSHEADS
Barrel	35 (wine)	1	
Butt	125-160	2	
Firkin	9	¼	
Hogshead	63 (wine)		
Keg	5-10		
Peg	4½	⅛	
Pipe	110-140 (wine)		2
Puncheon	72 (beer); 120 (spirits)		
Quarter Cask	28		½
Tun	252		4

Brief History of Cups, Pots, and Urns	
Pottery and wooden cups and bowls come into use	prehistory
Liquid-tight bags are sewn from animal skins	prehistory
Bronze pots and cups are fashioned in Europe	1800 B.C.
Egyptians produce fine alabaster vases	1600 B.C.
Crude glass vessels are produced	1500 B.C.
Glass-blown cups and urns are introduced	30 B.C.
Well-crafted leather containers sealed with tar or wax are in use	1300
Lead crystal glass containers are produced	1674

Smoking Pipes

— PIPES AND TOBACCO —

Smoking pipes were in use long before tobacco was discovered. People in many parts of the world smoked various kinds of herbs for religious reasons as well as for the pleasure it afforded. Pipes have been made of clay, bone, bamboo, metal, gourds, the branches and roots of trees, and a mineral known as meerschaum. Today, the best pipes are said to be made of briar and meerschaum.

Tobacco is a plant native to the American continent. Smoking the rolled leaves of the tobacco plant in the form of a cigar was one of the more curious discoveries Columbus made as he observed the New World. Hernando Cortés was probably the first to bring tobacco to Europe as he presented tobacco seeds to his king, Charles V, early in the 16th century. Late in the 16th century, pipe smoking was a familiar sight throughout Europe. Sir Walter Raleigh was not the first Englishman to smoke. He was rather the first "man of note" to smoke and encourage smoking; he made pipe smoking fashionable.

ADHAM A tube pipe made from the tibia bone of a sheep. It is hollowed and open on both ends, the larger end acting as a bowl.

SIZE: 10 inches long

PLACE: Northwest Africa and Arab countries

TIME: 1000s

ALSATIAN A water pipe used for smoking tobacco. The bowl and reservoir are made of porcelain, the stem of wood, and the mouthpiece of ebonite. The reservoir sometimes holds brandy instead of water.

SIZE: 10 to 12 inches high

PLACE: Europe, especially France and Germany

TIME: 1600s

APPLE A pipe shape (see illustration).

AUTHOR A pipe shape (see illustration).

BENT A pipe shape (see illustration).

BILLIARD A pipe shape (see illustration).

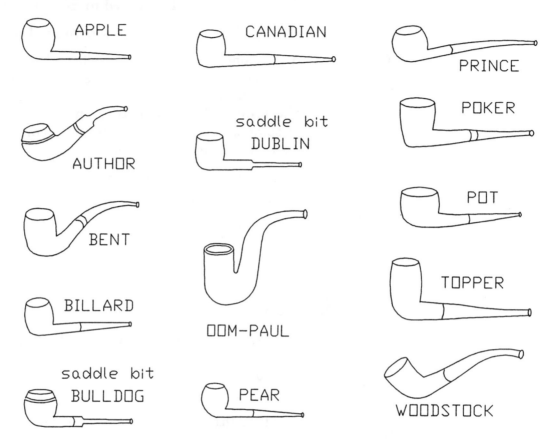

BRIAR A pipe bowl made from the root of the heath tree, native to most of Europe. A pipe made from this hard briar root is small, lightweight, hard wearing, and fire resistant, and gives a cool, sweet, mellow smoke. The first briar pipe was made in France, and it has become the favorite pipe among most smokers worldwide.

> PLACE: Europe, United States, and elsewhere

> TIME: Introduced in 1820s

BULLDOG A pipe shape (see illustration).

CALABASH A lightweight pipe made from the stem of a calabash gourd. Natives in South Africa were discovered cutting the neck from the gourd and making a pipe to smoke hemp. Through the years, Europeans improved the calabash pipe by training the neck of the gourd (which already has a natural bend) into a longer graceful crook as it is growing. An ebonite pipe stem was added to the end of the cut gourd, and the bowl was hollowed, enlarging it enough to receive a meerschaum insert so the charge of tobacco would not burn on the walls of the gourd. (See Meerschaum.) This is the pipe style that Arthur Conan Doyle chose to put into the hand of Sherlock Holmes.

SIZE: 9 inches long

PLACE AND TIME: Originated in South Africa - 1600s

Introduced to Europe - 1652

Improved with meerschaum insert - mid-1800s

CALUMET A ceremonial pipe, sometimes called a "peace pipe." The bowl is made of soft red stone, and the long stem is made of reed or ash wood. The pipe is decorated with carvings, horsehair, and bird feathers. It was smoked by most Plains tribes for a variety of spiritual reasons; sometimes as a symbol of peace and as a mark of welcome to strangers.

SIZE: 16 to 24 inches long

PLACE: North America (Indians)

TIME: Pre-colonial period

CANADIAN A pipe shape (see illustration).

CARROT A tobacco leaf tightly twisted into the shape of a large diameter carrot. The carrot was allowed to dry thoroughly and then rubbed on a snuff rasp to produce a coarse homemade tobacco powder.

CHERRYWOOD Any pipe that has been made from the branch of a wild cherry tree.

CHIBOUK A pipe made of several tight-fitting segments that simply slip together. The bowl is made of red clay and the stem of wood. The mouthpiece may be made of amber, bone, or tortoise shell. The mouth of the bowl may be funnel-shaped or covered with an iron lid. The entire length of the pipe is usually ornamented with decorative cords loosely connecting the various parts of the pipe.

SIZE: 20 to 26 inches

PLACE: Turkey

TIME: 1600s

CHUB A pipe shape (see illustration).

CHURCHWARDEN A long-stemmed pipe, originally made of clay. The clay churchwarden is still available, but the popular shape may also be purchased in briar with a long ebonite stem.

SIZE: 10 to 12 inches

PLACE: England

TIME: 1800s

CIGARETTE A quantity of finely shredded tobacco rolled in rice paper. Cigarette smoking was first popular in Turkey. It was known in Europe in the late 1700s, but cigarette smoking was not a common practice until soldiers from France and England met with the Turks during the Crimean War. Cigarettes were handmade till late in the 19th century, when a cigarette-making machine was perfected. In America production of popular brands began in 1910.

TIME AND PLACE: Turkey - 1800s

Europe - 1840s

United States - 1880s

CLAY PIPE A pipe made of terra cotta, wet clay, or ceramic. (See Chibouk, Churchwarden, Gambier, and Porcelain.) The mound-building Indians of America used clay to make many of their pipes.

CORNCOB A pipe made from the cob of an ear of Collier corn. This special hybrid of corn was developed for its exceptionally large and firm cob. The bowl is made from a cob at least two inches in diameter and can be fitted with a stem made of metal, wood, or hard rubber.

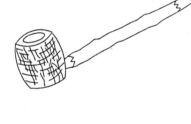

SIZE: 7 inches long

PLACE: South Central United States

TIME: Introduced in 1869

DOTTLE The caked ash that remains in a pipe after it has been smoked.

DUBLIN A pipe shape (see illustration).

EBONITE A hard, vulcanized black rubber used for the mouthpieces and stems of pipes.

GAMBIER A pipe made entirely of clay. It is mass-produced by a slip-casting process and is very inexpensive. The bowl is small, and the stem is very fragile. The pipe is so brittle it is almost impossible to carry in a pocket.

SIZE: 8 to 10 inches long

PLACE: England

TIME: Late 1800s

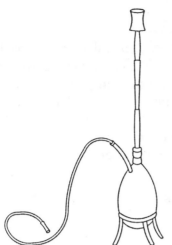

HOOKAH An Oriental water pipe made of metal or pottery. A charge of tobacco is loaded into the bowl on the top of the pipe. When lit, the smoke is drawn through a water bath and a flexible tube. The hookah is too large and heavy to hold in the hands comfortably. It is mounted on a stand because of its weight.

SIZE: 3 feet high; tube is 3 to 4 feet long

PLACE: India

TIME: Late 1700s

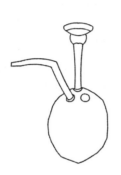

HUBBLE-BUBBLE An English nickname for the water pipe of India. This pipe is made of a coconut shell. The pipe bowl is loaded with tobacco or other smokeable herb, and the long stem inserted into one of the eyes of the coconut and plunged into the liquid of the reservoir. A flexible tube is inserted into another of the eyes so the smoker can draw the cooled and filtered smoke into his mouth. (See also Narghile and Hookah.)

SIZE: 6 inches in diameter

PLACE: East India

TIME: Nickname given in 1800s

JACOB A Gambier (see Gambier) pipe bowl that has the shape of the head of a bearded man. This more carefully crafted clay pipe may be designed to accept a wood stem and an ebonite mouthpiece.

SIZE: 8 to 10 inches long

PLACE: England

TIME: Late 1800s

MEERSCHAUM A soft, light, heat-resisting magnesium silicate mined in Asia Minor, used almost entirely in Turkey for making pipe bowls. At first, the hand-carved meerschaum pipe was very expensive and only the wealthy could afford to own one. By the end of the 19th century, it was being mass produced in Austria and became more widely available. The meerschaum pipe bowl, after all these years, is still considered to be superior to a pipe made of any other substance.

PLACE: Turkey

TIME: 1750 to the present

MULL A snuff container made from a ram's horn. Some mulls have flattened bottoms or small legs so they may be set on a table. Smaller mulls are designed to be carried in the user's pocket. The mull is fitted with a lid of bone, ivory, or metal and is sometimes decorated with carvings. The small end is artificially carved into a tight curve.

SIZE: 3 to 5 inches long

PLACE: Scotland

TIME: Late 1800s

NARGHILE A handheld water pipe, originally made from a whole coconut. The refined narghile was made of porcelain, metal, or clay but the coconut shape was retained. (See also Hubble-Bubble and Water Pipe.)

SIZE: 18 inches high

PLACE: Persia

TIME: Late 1800s

NOSE WARMER A pipe that has the mouthpiece connected directly to the bowl. The stem is nearly nonexistent.

OOM PAUL A pipe shape (see illustration).

PEACE PIPE A ceremonial pipe of the Plains Indians of America. (See Calumet.)

PEAR A pipe shape (see illustration).

POKER A pipe shape (see illustration).

PORCELAIN A pipe bowl made of cast ceramic clay. Porcelain has largely replaced clay in the bowl of the Gambier since it is so much more durable. A new porcelain pipe has a baked glaze finish, and the surface is highly polished. As the pipe ages and is exposed to repeated overheating, a network of tiny cracks appears in the surface of the bowl.

POT BOWL A pipe shape (see illustration).

PRINCE A pipe shape (see illustration).

SCROW A bag for storing and shipping large quantities of tobacco. The bag is made of a buffalo skin. The pelt is folded over onto itself and sewn up both sides. The raw side of the hide is turned out, and the fur inside is in contact with the tobacco.

PLACE: America

TIME: 1700s

SNUFF A preparation of powdered tobacco to be taken up the nose. Snuff was introduced to the French court at about the time that the English court became aware of pipe smoking. In the next hundred years a variety of snuff mixes became available, including some that were mixed with perfume.

PLACE AND TIME: Introduced in France - mid-1500s

In general use in all of Europe - mid-1600s to 1800s

SNUFF BOX A container to carry a personal supply of snuff. Most boxes are small enough to be carried in a pocket, but larger boxes were made. The master of a home places the larger box on a desk or table and shares his favorite blend with his guests. The snuff box came to be an art object, magnificently carved and painted. The box and a gold-headed cane were the professional equipment of a physician. Many were crafted in precious metals   the snuff box was an object to show.

SIZE: 2½ inches long, 1½ inches wide, ½ inch thick

PLACE: Europe, especially England and France

TIME: 1600s

SNUFF RASP A fine-toothed rasp for making a coarse variety of snuff. As the tobacco stick or Carrot (see Carrot) is rubbed over the grater, the powder falls through holes and collects in a receptacle below. Some rasps are made to be carried and used as a snuff box; others were intended for the owner to empty the contents into another container. In the 17th to 18th centuries grating one's own snuff was mostly confined to the poorer classes, yet judging from the finely engraved rasps, the practice evidently saw some use in higher circles.

SIZE: 3½ inches long, 2 inches wide, ¾ inch thick

PLACE: Europe

TIME: 1600s to 1700s

TOBAGO A small "Y"-shaped tube made of reed or cane for sniffing powdered tobacco or the smoke from burning tobacco directly into both nostrils. Christopher Columbus discovered the tobago in use by the natives of San Domingo.

TOMAHAWK PEACE PIPE
A pipe made by Europeans for trade with the American Indians. The English, French, and Spaniards each had their own design for this war club, and they hoped the Indians would use it to help them as they fought against the other Europeans for supremacy in the New World.

SIZE: 1½ feet long

PLACE: United States

TIME: Early 1700s

TOPPER
A pipe shape (see illustration).

TUBE PIPE
Any pipe that is designed with the bowl and pipe stem in a continuous straight line. This pipe can be made of bamboo, reed, bone, pottery, stone, or metal tubing.

TOUBA
A Moorish pipe with a small bowl made of wood and a stem made from a piece of copper tube.

WATER PIPE
Any pipe with two compartments, one being a bowl to contain the burning tobacco (or narcotic) and the other to hold a reservoir of water. The smoke from the bowl passes through a water bath in the lower part of the pipe before it enters the flexible stem to the smoker's lips. The water cools the smoke to room temperature and filters out some of the tobacco flakes and impurities.

WOODSTOCK
A pipe shape (see illustration).

Brief History of Smoking and Tobacco

Pipes are used for smoking dried herbs, hemp, or tobacco	unknown early date
Cortés brings tobacco samples and seeds to Spain	1518
Snuff is introduced to France	1550
Tobacco is introduced to the court of England	1558
Calabash pipe is introduced to Europe	1652
Turkey develops the chibouk	1600s
Snuff is in general use	1600s to 1800s
Meerschaum is mined and carved for pipe bowls	1750
Clay churchwarden pipe is developed	1800s
First briar pipe is developed	1820s
Corncob pipe is developed	1869
Cigarettes are in common use	mid-1800s

Games

---------------------------------- GAMBLING ----------------------------------

There is little doubt (even though there is little evidence) that games are as old as man himself. Races and competitions of strength were probably the first sort of games. Games involving targets probably came next. It is not unreasonable to suppose that the spectators had favorites among the rivals, nor that they would back up their preferences with a wager.

In another game that dates from antiquity, lots were cast and players bet on the chance result. A stick with two flat sides was the first gaming piece. It was flipped in the air much as we would flip a coin. Somewhat later, but still in an undefined early period of antiquity, board games were produced, pitting markers in a simulated race around a track. The track was drawn in the dirt, and the speed was determined by a throw of the sticks. Such games include Pachisi and the rudimentary beginnings of Backgammon.

Six-sided dice in the form of bones and terra cotta cubes were found entombed in the Pyramid of Cheops in 3000 B.C. Egypt. These are the first relics we have of gaming pieces.

The major developments in gambling—dice, the lottery, the wheel, everything in fact except cards—were in place and functioning before the times of the Greeks and Romans. All the elaborations that followed have just been variations on these basic original themes.

Since the times of the Greeks and Romans, a large body of recorded evidence of gambling comes to us in a rather negative way—in the form of prohibitions. A continuous stream of laws has been written over the years offering harsh penalties to discourage the sloth and poverty that accompany an over-attention to gaming.

ALQUERQUE A board game consisting of a geometric matrix where players capture opposing men by jumping the pieces. The forerunner of checkers. (See Checkers.)

PLACE: Egypt

TIME: 1400 B.C.

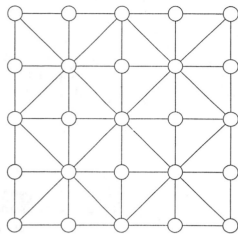

ASTRAGAL An ankle bone from a sheep—one of the very first dice. The astragal is flat on four sides and was useful in throwing lots.

ATEP A guessing game where one predicts the number of fingers or sticks extended by his opponent. (See Mora.)

PLACE: India

ATOUTS A set of 21, 22, or 36 picture cards (the number depends on the manufacturing artist) used in fortune-telling and also as trumps in the games played with tarot cards. (See Tarot Cards.)

BRIDGE DECK A deck of 52 cards (no joker) used for playing bridge and similar games in which the player must hold many cards in his hand at one time. (Compare with Poker Deck.)

SIZE: Card - 2¼ inches wide, 3½ inches high

CARDS The earliest playing card was made of oiled paper. It developed in Korea but quickly journeyed to China to become popular as a game-playing and fortune-telling device. Many variations of the Chinese deck were made in this early stage of development. A deck of 120 cards consists of 4 suits with 30 cards each; a deck of 80 has 10 cards in 8 suits. The narrow strips were held and manipulated by the top edge and hung down stiffly. There are many other combinations. The cards in the illustration are wider and date from 1300 A.D.

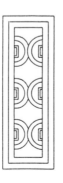

SIZE: ½ inch wide, 7 inches long

PLACE: China

TIME: 100 A.D.

The playing cards of India were developed at about the same time as the cards of China. The Indian cards, however, are round. There are either 8 or 10 suits, each suit consisting of 12 cards—10 number cards and 2 court or face cards. The suits are patterned after the characters or animals found in the Hindu myths of the period, and each suit is painted in its own vivid color.

SIZE: 1½ inches in diameter

PLACE: India

TIME: 100 A.D.

It is not perfectly clear how cards were introduced to Europe, but with the migration their size and shape changed again. The cards designed by artists in Europe were printed on heavy paper and were a lot like our present pasteboard playing cards.

Playing cards appeared in all countries of Europe at about the same time. They were distributed by merchants, wandering fortune-telling gypsies, and soldiers. The artists of each country designed face cards and selected suits to reflect their own nation and its culture. Tarot playing cards were popular in France, Italy, Germany, and Spain. In the next 25 years, games were invented for the 52-card deck, the atout pictures (used primarily in foretelling the future) were discarded, and the card deck traveled to England.

SIZE: 3 inches wide, 7 inches long

PLACE AND TIME: France, Italy, Germany, Spain - 1390s

England - early 1400s

CARD GAMES Most card games fall into four classifications:

1. The object is to collect specific arrangements of cards, either in a straight run or in groups of the same numeric value. Rummy, canasta, and poker are games of this type.

2. The goal is the taking of tricks. Games in this category include bridge, whist, and hearts.

3. The features of classifications 1 and 2 are combined: the player melds his combinations for a score and then collects the cards into his hand and replays them in an effort to take tricks. Pinochle and the 400-year-old piquet are games of this sort.

4. The player is pitted against a "bank." He bets that he can guess an upcoming card or that he can come closer to a predetermined number of points than the dealer. Baccarat, blackjack, red dog, and faro are examples of games in this category.

CHECKERS A game of skill for two players, using a board exactly like a chess board. Each player uses 12 pieces and the moves and method of capturing the opponent's pieces are taken from an ancient Egyptian game called Alquerque (see Alquerque).

PLACE: Introduced in France

TIME: Early 1100s to the present

CHESS A game of skill played by two persons on a board divided into 64 squares. Each player has 16 pieces; each piece has its own prescribed pattern of moving. The goal is to capture the opponent's king.

The origin of chess is somewhat obscure, but there is general agreement that it began in India as a war game called *Shaturanga.* It was known in Persia as *Shatranj,* and it was here that the rules and the names of the pieces were set down for the first time. The Danish raiders are credited with introducing the game to England. Each nation of players had its own "house rules," and in 1900 the rules were standardized by an international committee.

PLACE AND TIME: India - 500s

Persia - 600s

China - 700s

Europe - 700 to 900

England - 1000s

Worldwide - to the present

COURT CARD A high-count face card in a deck of cards. These picture cards are also called "honor cards." The contemporary cards in America are jack, queen, king, and ace. Court cards of the past have included such characters as knave, varlet, knight, dame, duke, duchess, cavalier, and others.

CRAPS An American gambling game played with two dice. Craps is perhaps the most popular casino game.

PLACE: Introduced in Louisiana

TIME: 1800s to the present

DICE A pair of six-sided cubes with a number of dots from one to six engraved on each face of the cube and used for gambling.

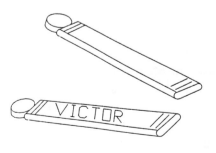

Dice have evolved over the millennia from the earliest beginnings of mankind. They were made of carved wood, plum and peach seeds with the sides ground flat, walnut shells, pottery, deer horn, bones, and stones. Later they were refined and made from bronze, ivory, and marble. An early set of bone dice is pictured.

An early game was played with a two-sided stick that could fall onto the ground in only two ways. The next development was to make a heavier stick with four flat sides. Finally, the stick was cut into cubes so any of six sides may come to the top with equal frequency.

Today there are several grades of dice manufactured ranging from the inexpensive "dime store" variety to the well-balanced dice for casino play.

DOMINOES A domino is a rectangular tile made up of two square fields. Each field is imprinted with dots from one to six, just like the markings found on dice. Some domino games are played by matching fields with the same number of dots. Another popular game involves totalling the number of dots on the exposed ends. The tiles can be arranged in suits, and they can be dealt and played like cards in games where tricks are taken. Although dominoes may appear to be the offspring of a union between dice and cards, they are centuries older. Relics that look like our present-day dominoes have been dug up in Ur of the Chaldea, dating to 2500 B.C. The games outlined above were invented 300 years ago.

PLACE: Introduced in Europe, especially France and England

TIME: Late 1700s to the present

DRAUGHTS British. The game of checkers (see Checkers).

EUCHRE A game using a 32-card deck — all cards ranking below seven are removed, the ace is high. Five cards are dealt, an upturned card determines trump, and points are given for the number of tricks taken. Euchre is of American origin and enjoyed great popularity before poker was introduced.

PLACE: United States

TIME: Late 1700s

HAZARD An early game of chance played with two dice, from which craps (see Craps) is derived.

LANTERLOO (Also Loo.) A card game played by six or seven players. Three cards are dealt and then played in an attempt to take tricks. Each trick wins one-third of the pot. Any player not winning any tricks must put up an ante for the next pot.

PLACE: England and United States

TIME: 1800s

MORA A game played by two people standing back to back. The object of the game is to guess the number of fingers extended by the other player. A third neutral person acts as a score-keeping referee.

PLACE AND TIME: China - 1000 B.C.

Rome - 100 B.C.

OMBRE A card game played by three players with a deck of 40 cards. It was one of the very earliest card games. Ombre is a rather complex game that is played somewhat like whist (see Whist). The complexity is in the ranking of the cards—if a red suit is trump the ranking is as follows: ace of spades, seven of trump, ace of clubs, ace of trump, then king, queen, jack, then deuce, 3, 4, 5, and finally 6 of trump is the lowest card. Whew! It is no surprise that whist would become popular when a choice could be made. Ombre was popular in England, giving way to whist when it came along.

PLACE AND TIME: Spain - 1500s

England - 1600 to 1700

PACHISI An ancient game for four players. The moves of markers around a board were determined by the throwing of cowrie shells.

PLACE: India

PIQUET A game using 36 cards. It is the forerunner of euchre (see Euchre).

PIQUET DECK A modified deck of cards used for playing several games, including piquet, euchre, and whist. The sixteen lowest numbered cards, the 2's, 3's, 4's, and 5's are all removed, making a deck of 36.

POKER A card game intended for gambling. The exact origin is unknown, but it is clear that when poker appeared in America it quickly found a home on the Mississippi river boats. An early version of the game was played with only twenty cards—the 12 picture face cards, the aces, and the tens. The game now uses a 53-card deck (standard plus joker) and involves collecting cards of the same denomination, or suit, or a total of five cards in a sequence. The highest hand is a five-card sequence with the ace high, all in the same suit.

PLACE AND TIME: Introduced to America - early 1800s

A set of rules published - 1834

POKER DECK A deck of 53 cards, including the joker. (Compare with Bridge Deck.)

SIZE: 2½ inches wide, 3½ inches high

ROULETTE A game for gambling, evolving to its present form from another game of chance, the wheel. Players bet chips on a matrix of 37 squares. The winning number is selected when a spinning ball falls into one of the 37 spokes of a stationary wheel.

PLACE: Introduced in France

TIME: 1780s

SHAH-MAT A board game and ancestor to the game of chess.

PLACE: Persia

TIME: 500s B.C.

SUIT A set of 13 related playing cards, four suits making a deck of 52 cards. The contemporary cards in America have suits of clubs, diamonds, hearts, and spades. The suits used in the past could have any of several names depending on the country in which they were manufactured. Objects used to distinguish the suits have included cups, batons, swords, pentacles, wands, books, birds, money, roses, acorns, bells, leaves, pikes, trefoils, tiles, hounds, stags, ducks, falcons, and others.

TAROT CARDS An early deck of cards. The tarot deck had 22 (more or less) beautifully painted picture cards called atouts. When the atouts are added to the 56 suit cards, the complete deck has 78 tarot cards. Tarot cards were used for fortune-telling and for several card games.

PLACE: Introduced in Europe

TIME: 1300s to the present

WHIST A forerunner of bridge, it has many of the same rules. The goal of the game is to collect tricks. There is no bidding; trump is decided as the last card dealt is turned face up. The person to the dealer's left begins play. All players take turns playing a card in an attempt to play the highest card, winning the trick. Anyone who is not able to follow suit in any round may trump, highest trump winning the trick. *A Treatise on the Game of Whist* was published by Hoyle in 1742.

PLACE: England and United States

TIME: 1700s to 1800s

Brief History of Gambling

Races and competitions of strength	prehistory
Casting lots	prehistory
Simulated race—a board game	prehistory
Dice in the Pyramid of Cheops	3000 B.C.
Egyptians play a board game, Alquerque	1400 B.C.
Most forms of gambling—lottery, wheel, dice—are in place and functioning	500 B.C.
Playing cards are introduced in China and India	100 A.D.
Chess is developed	500 to 1000
Checkers is developed	1100
Tarot playing cards are developed in Europe	1300s
Card games are developed using the 52-card deck	1400
American dice game, craps, is developed	1800s
Poker is developed in the United States	early 1800s
Bridge is developed from whist	1850

TOYS

It is likely that the earliest children's toys—marbles and tops—were inherited from the world of adults. These articles, made to seek the will of the gods and to foretell the future, fell into young hands when their elders cast them aside.

In the middle of the 19th century, the industrial revolution caught up with the toymaker. Until this time all toys were handmade. Some of the ones we see preserved in museums are fine examples of folk art.

The list below includes name brand toys manufactured in the United States.

Brief History of Toys	
Marbles—an adult's divining stones become a child's toy	3000 B.C.
Tops—Whirling tops are made of clay in Babylonia	3000 B.C.
Yo-yo is invented in China	1000 B.C.
Donald Duncan markets the Duncan yo-yo	1924
Kite is first flown in China	200 B.C.
Fireworks—skyrockets and firecrackers invented in China	1000
Jigsaw puzzle is concurrently invented in France and England	1700s
Roller skates are invented and introduced in London	1759
Mah-jong is created and introduced in China	1850
Teddy Bear—a doll for Roosevelt's son is marketed by Ideal Toys	1900
Bagatelle—a table game with punched holes and ball bearings, the forerunner of pinball machines, is introduced	1920s
Pinball—an improved bagatelle game is developed by Gottlieb	1930
Gottlieb, Ballyhoo, and Mills market pinball machines	early 1930s
battery-operated pinball is replaced by 110V plug-in model	1935
Gottlieb introduces flippers	1947
Monopoly—a game of real estate is invented	1933
Slinky—a high-tech spring is marketed as a toy	1940s
Silly Putty—a plastic age by-product is marketed as a toy	1947
Frisbee is invented by some students at Yale University	1947
marketed by Wham-O	1968
Scrabble—a crossword puzzle game is introduced	1948
Hula Hoop is invented and marketed by Wham-O	1958
Barbie Doll is made by Mattel	1958
Ken	1961
Video games—Pong—first animated home video game is introduced by Atari	1972
Space Invaders—an early electronic arcade game is introduced	1978
Pac-Man is the king of video games	1983
Dungeons and Dragons is introduced	1973
Rubik's Cube is invented by Erno Rubix of Hungary	1979
Cabbage Patch doll is available for "adoption"	1983

Furniture

——— BATHROOM ———

The bathtub, the indoor toilet, and the use of sewers and plumbing systems all have individual histories going back to early times. Recent excavations in Scotland have uncovered evidence to suggest that the residents of the area had indoor plumbing that could remove waste from their homes and dump it into a nearby stream as early as 8000 B.C. Indications show that similar sewage systems were in operation in other parts of the world: in Pakistan - 3000 B.C., in Crete - 2000 B.C., and in Egypt - 1500 B.C.

In the past, medicinal baths using minerals and salt water were equally as popular as baths taken to cleanse the body. The bath peaked in popularity with the Roman public bath houses, which were in vogue from 200 B.C. to 200 A.D. The bathroom and all its niceties fell with the Roman Empire, remaining lost for 1400 years. The modern bathroom and its fixtures were slowly reintroduced beginning in the 1600s.

BASIN STAND   A small table or stand with a circular hole cut into the top to accept a wash basin. The stand is used for washing and shaving the face.

PLACE: Introduced in England

TIME: Introduced in 1700s

BIDET   A low stool with four legs and an open seat containing a metal or earthenware bowl. This bathroom fixture is straddled and used for bathing the genitals.

PLACE: Europe, particularly France

TIME: Introduced in late 1800s

CAST IRON BATHTUB   A white porcelain enameled tub with a rolled rim and claw and ball feet. Hot and cold running water is available with this tub.

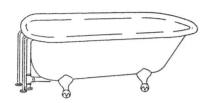

PLACE: Europe and United States

TIME: Early 1900s

CHAMBER POT A crockery pot stored in a Commode (see Commode) or under a bed to be used as a night-time toilet.

Another kind of chamber pot consisted of a metal pail with a wire handle and a tight-fitting lid.

PLACE: Europe and United States

TIME: Mid-1800s to 1930s

CLOSE CHAIR A bedroom chair having a deep apron on the front to hide a chamber pot. The seat is raised or removed when the chair is in use. A more rustic version is a simple boxed stool and has no chair back.

PLACE: England and United States

TIME: Mid-1800s

COMMODE A cabinet containing a chamber pot, used in rural districts before sewage systems were installed. The pail is removed and emptied daily.

PLACE: England and United States

TIME: Late 1800s

FLUSH TOILET A porcelain bowl connected to a wooden flush tank. When the tank, located near the ceiling, is flushed, a rush of running water siphons wastes from the toilet bowl.

The style of toilet with the low tank familiar to most of us was introduced in the early 1900s.

PLACE: Europe and United States

TIME: Late 1800s to early 1900s

HIP BATH A sheet-metal tub with a scooped backrest rising above the rim. Used from Victorian times for bathing the entire body.

PLACE: England and United States

TIME: Late 1800s

SITZ TUB   A bath tub. Same as Hip Bath (see Hip Bath).

SLIPPER BATH   A sheet-metal bathtub whose shape resembles that of a footprint.

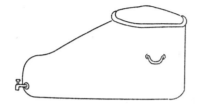

PLACE: Europe, particularly France and England

TIME: 1700s

A deeper, covered bathtub that actually looks like a slipper-shoe is used for prolonged periods of soaking. Benjamin Franklin brought a bathtub of this style to the United States from France.

PLACE: Europe, particularly France and England

TIME: Late 1700s

WATER CLOSET   A Flush Toilet (see Flush Toilet). The term was prevalent in the United States till the early 1900s and is still in use in England.

BEDS

For many thousands of years, people throughout the world have slept on pallets made of leaves or straw laid on a bare floor. Early on, pallets were covered with animal skins or woolen blankets to make them smoother and more comfortable. In the Middle Ages, the coverings were sewn together, and a mattress was made by stuffing the sack with straw or feathers. The bed was rolled up during the day if floor space was at a premium. If there was plenty of room, a low box was built to contain the loose straw. For most of the world's population this was enough.

The notion of complicating the sleeping quarters with a bedstead was for a long time widely looked on as unnecessary or perhaps even impractical. However, 3000 years ago the Egyptians had wooden bed frames raised on legs carved in the form of animal feet. And excavations at Pompeii have disclosed bed frames made of bronze. There have always been those who appreciate luxury when they can afford it.

CAMP BED   A portable bed for domestic use with canopy and curtains hanging on all four sides of the frame. The camp bed of the 18th and 19th centuries was quite elaborate and not at all as simple as the name may imply. (See also Field Bed.)

STYLE: Sheraton

PLACE: England

TIME: Early 1800s

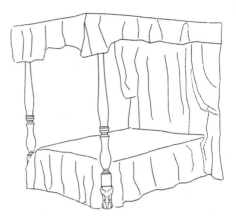

CANOPY BED A bed covered by a drapery, a hood, or an awning. A canopied bed with surrounding draperies provides the owner privacy, a sense of opulence, and freedom from insects. It is likely that the Knights of the Crusades brought the designs from the Middle East to Europe.

In the 17th century, both France and England made excessive use of fabric in the hangings of the canopy. The draperies were very full, and wooden panels were completely concealed in the folds of fabric. (See Tester Bed.)

PLACE AND TIME: Persia, Greece, and Rome - 200 B.C. to 1200s

Introduced to England and France - 1200s

DUCHESSE BED A canopied couch. The canopy has the same dimensions as the couch beneath but is supported at the headboard only.

PLACE: France

TIME: Early 1600s

FIELD BED A portable canopied bed. It is furnished with hardware that will knock apart or fold so the unit can be moved from place to place as needed. Officers actually took these beds into the field on military campaigns.

PLACE: France and England

TIME: 1600s

FOUR POSTER A bed with long posts, one at each corner of the frame. It is an outgrowth of the wall-mounted tester bed. Originally the posts were necessary to support a canopy. From the 19th century to the present the canopy was likely to be omitted.

STYLE: Elizabethan

PLACE: Originated in England

TIME: Late 1500s to the present

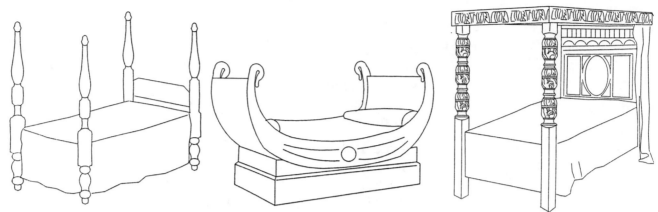

From left to right, Four poster, Sleigh bed, Tester bed.

SLEIGH BED   A bed with a large headboard having the shape of a one-horse open sleigh. The design came from France but the name came from America.

STYLE: French Empire

PLACE: France and United States

TIME: Mid-1800s

TENT BED   An enclosed canopy bed that forms a small chamber within the bedroom. With the curtains drawn closed, this bed looks somewhat like a Persian tent.

TESTER BED   A canopied bed. The tester can be made of lightweight fabric or heavy wooden paneling. In the 15th century, the tester was hung from the ceiling or attached to the wall adjacent to the bed. In Elizabethan times, the bed became free-standing and the tester was attached to the bed posts.

PLACE: France and England

TIME: 1400s

BENCHES AND SOFAS

ANTIMACASSAR   A doily or other detachable covering to protect the backs of armchairs and sofas from soiling by wear or contact with the hair. Macassar oil lost its popularity as a hair dressing at the end of the 19th century, but the antimacassar retained its popularity as an ornamental feature into the mid-1900s.

PLACE: United States

TIME: Mid-1800s

BANQUETTE   An upholstered bench with a back and no arms, especially one placed alongside the wall of a restaurant.

PLACE: France

TIME: Late 1600s

CANAPE A small sofa, usually intended to accommodate two persons. The distinguishing feature of this sofa is the sweeping curve that is formed as the arms join the back.

STYLE: Louis XIV

PLACE: Introduced in France, spread throughout Europe

TIME: Late 1600s

CASSAPANCA An all-wood settee formed by adding arms and back to an ornately carved chest. (See Chests—Cassapanca.)

PLACE: Italy

TIME: 1500s

CHAISE LONGUE A chair whose seat is elongated to support the sitter's outstretched legs. The chaise longue is distinct from a sofa in that there is no back and that one end is left open.

PLACE: France

TIME: Late 1700s

CHESTERFIELD A large overstuffed sofa or couch with pillowed and tufted upholstering and rounded ends the same height as the back. The upholstery is styled after the Turkish ottoman. This sofa is named either after an Earl of Chesterfield or the Chesterfield district where it was made, but in either case it was introduced in Victorian England.

PLACE: England

TIME: Late 1800s

CONFIDANTE A small sofa made by designing two or even three armchairs into a single piece of furniture. Although the confidante seems to place divisions between the participants, the barriers are low and an intimacy is retained.

PLACE: England

TIME: Late 1700s

COUCH A piece of furniture having a back and one or two ends. The term is generic and refers to any piece on which several persons could be seated or on which one could recline.

DAVENPORT BED A large upholstered sofa that may be unfolded to form a bed.

> PLACE: United States
>
> TIME: Early 1900s

DAYBED A chair with an elongated seat to accommodate the sitter's out-stretched legs. The daybed is the forerunner of the sofa and includes rest beds and chaise longues.

> PLACE: Introduced in France, spread throughout Europe
>
> TIME: Mid-1600s

DIVAN A long, low upholstered bench, without arm rests or back.

DUCHESSE A double-ended daybed formed by placing two upholstered armchairs and a matching stool together to make one piece of furniture. The three-piece sectional is sometimes equipped with hooks and staples to keep the pieces from shifting.

> STYLE: Louis XV
>
> PLACE: France
>
> TIME: Mid-1700s

LECTUS A couch equally suited for lounging, dining, or sleeping. The lectus is liberally provided with cushions.

> PLACE: Rome
>
> TIME: 100 to 200 A.D.

LOUNGE A daybed with a heavily padded headrest. The lounge may be thought of as an easy chair with an elongated seat to support the legs.

LOVE SEAT A small sofa where two people can sit intimately together. The backs are sometimes built on opposite sides of the sofa so the couple sit side by side but facing each other. (See Confidante.)

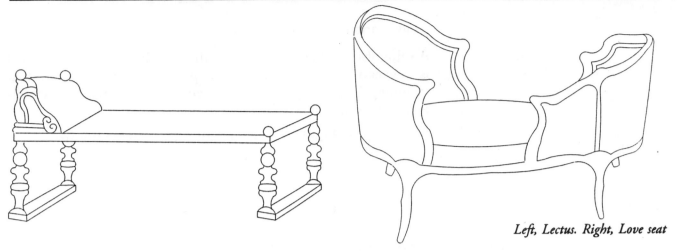

Left, Lectus. Right, Love seat

MERIDIENNE A sofa distinguished by the fact that the arm on one end is higher than the other. The back joins the two ends in a gentle curve.

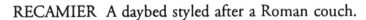

STYLE: French Empire

PLACE: France

TIME: Early 1800s

RECAMIER A daybed styled after a Roman couch.

STYLE: Directoire

PLACE: France

TIME: Early 1800s

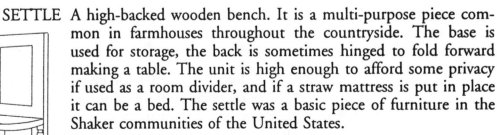

SETTEE A seat with a back and arms about twice the width of a chair, just large enough for two people to sit comfortably side by side. It is a small sofa and almost always has the seating surface upholstered.

SETTLE A high-backed wooden bench. It is a multi-purpose piece common in farmhouses throughout the countryside. The base is used for storage, the back is sometimes hinged to fold forward making a table. The unit is high enough to afford some privacy if used as a room divider, and if a straw mattress is put in place it can be a bed. The settle was a basic piece of furniture in the Shaker communities of the United States.

PLACE AND TIME: Medieval Europe - 1200s

Tudor England - 1500s

Shaker America - 1800s

SOFA Any seat for two or three persons that has a fixed back and arms on each end. The sofa is designed for comfort and is usually padded and upholstered.

WINDOW SEAT   An upholstered bench with ends that act as arm rests. The seat is low enough and the ends are spaced far enough apart that incoming light is not obscured even when the bench is set directly in front of a window.

PLACE: Introduced in England, spread throughout Europe

TIME: Early 1700s

CABINETS AND CUPBOARDS

ALMIRAH   An Anglo-Indian term applied to all types of cupboards.

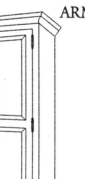

AMBRY   A storage cabinet with doors. With ventilated grillwork doors, the ambry was the first pantry.

PLACE: Europe

TIME: 1400s

ARMOIRE   A large, sometimes massive cabinet, cupboard, or wardrobe with two doors. The armoire is frequently highly decorated with panels, mouldings, and carvings.

SIZE: 7 to 9 feet tall

PLACE: Originated in France

TIME: Introduced in late 1600s

CELLARET   A lockable cabinet (or deep drawer in a cabinet) fitted with a bottle rack to store liquor and wine. The cellaret was an early-day liquor cabinet.

STYLE: Georgian

PLACE: England

TIME: Mid-1700s

CHIFFONIER A tall, narrow cabinet or chest of drawers fitted with two open book shelves. The working surface was used for writing or sewing. (Compare with Secretary.)

PLACE: France

TIME: Late 1700s

CLOTHES PRESS A cabinet, closet, or wardrobe for storing clothing.

COMMODE A term originally used to refer to a chest of drawers for the storage of folded clothing.

PLACE AND TIME: France - early 1700s

England - mid-1700s

Later the term referred to a nightstand containing a chamber pot.

PLACE: England and United States

TIME: Late 1800s

CORNER CUPBOARD A china cupboard designed to occupy the corner of a room. The first corner cupboards hung from the wall, but free-standing cupboards soon became popular.

PLACE: England

TIME: Early 1700s

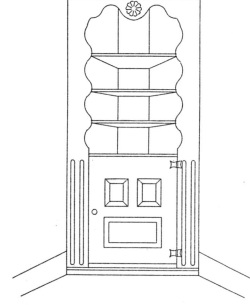

COURT CUPBOARD A cupboard for storing and displaying plates, cups, and dinnerware. The cabinet is constructed with two levels: the upper section is a recessed cabinet with drawers; the lower section may be enclosed with doors or it may be uncovered, exposing a lower shelf called a pot board.

STYLE: Tudor

PLACE: England

TIME: 1500s

CREDENZA A counter-height cupboard with drawers, used to prepare and serve food. The Italian credenza was a heavy piece of furniture purposely reflecting the architectural style of the 15th century.

STYLE: Renaissance

PLACE: Originated in Italy

TIME: 1400s to the present

CUPBOARD A cabinet used to store and display drinking cups and dining plates. The term is generic and has come to describe any cabinet with doors where household articles such as dishes, foodstuffs, linens, or clothing are stored.

PLACE: Originated in Europe

TIME: Originated in 1300s

DOLE CUPBOARD A cabinet used in a church to store food that is intended for distribution to the poor. It sometimes hangs from a wall and some dole cupboards are built to be free-standing.

HIGHBOY An American name for the English tallboy, a chest mounted on another chest. Sometimes the upper chest was mounted on a lowboy (see Lowboy) in which case the unit had legs.

PLACE AND TIME: Originated in Holland and England - late 1600s

United States - early 1700s

HUTCH A chest or cabinet, with doors, for storing food. The doors of a hutch are always ventilated, sometimes with a simple grating and sometimes with very intricate pierced decoration modeled after tracery found in gothic windows. (See also Ambry.)

PLACE: Originated in Italy and France

TIME: Originated in 1200s

KAS A massive cabinet with large, heavily paneled doors used to store a variety of possessions. In the bedroom it is used as a wardrobe, but it is just as likely to be found in the dining room as storage for plates and utensils. The kas was common in the

Dutch American colonies of New England.

PLACE: Holland

TIME: 1600s

LINEN PRESS A linen closet or large upright cupboard with shelves for storing sheets, towels, and tablecloths. Another more literal meaning refers to a 17th to 18th century "press" consisting of a frame, two boards, and a large wooden screw that would remove wrinkles from linens.

LIVERY CUPBOARD A well-ventilated cupboard for storing food. (See Hutch.)

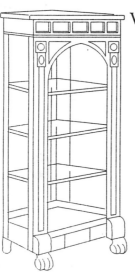

LOWBOY A chest of one long drawer and two or three shorter ones mounted on legs to be table height. The lowboy was used in the bedroom for clothing storage, with its flat working space often serving as a dressing table.

PLACE: Originated in England and United States

TIME: Originated in mid-1700s

POT BOARD An open-bottomed shelf on a livery or cupboard to store pots.

TALLBOY The English term for a chest-on-chest. (See Highboy.)

VITRINE A glass display cabinet to show valuable or delicate curios. Glass doors were installed on existing cabinets in the late 1600s both to show and protect collected Oriental porcelain pieces, but a cabinet designed specifically for display purposes waited another hundred years.

PLACE: France and England

TIME: Late 1700s

CHAIRS AND STOOLS

More than any other single item of furniture, the chair reflects the owner's social and economic status and his taste in decoration. Through man's history, sitting places have gone through a tremendous range of styles. You find everything from a log, to a three-legged stool, to a throne, to the elegance of a Hepplewhite, to the modern chair that looks more like sculpture (in some cases requiring instructions from the designer to know just where he intends you to put yourself). Every fifty years or so a new major chair design has appeared on the scene. Recently, we have been so impatient with former fashions that this rate has increased. A significant new chair style is now being introduced each decade.

ARCADE BACK CHAIR

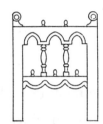

A chair back in the form of a series of arches. The top stretcher of the chair forms the pediments of the arches, and turned spindles form the columns.

PLACE: Derbyshire and Yorkshire districts of England

TIME: Late 1600s

ARROW BACK CHAIR

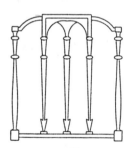

Any chair with an arrow motif in the spindles of the back. The spindles may be flat, with crude arrowheads pointing upward, or the spindle may have a delicate shaft with the arrowhead pointing down, as is the case in some of the Sheraton designs.

STYLE: Sheraton and others

PLACE: England

TIME: Early 1800s

BACK STOOL

A three-legged stool with a narrow slat backrest. A three-legged stool was especially practical on the uneven floors of its time. (See also Sgabello.)

PLACE: Europe, particularly Italy

TIME: Mid-1600s

BALLOON BACK CHAIR

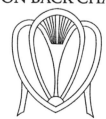

A chair back resembling a hot air balloon. (See also Shield Back Chair.) The chair back may have as many as three balloons intertwined. The two-balloon back chair is sometimes called a "heart back."

STYLE: Hepplewhite

PLACE: England

TIME: 1790s

BALUSTER BACK CHAIR   A chair back with a wide center splat resembling a flattened stair rail baluster. The baluster back is typical of the Queen Anne style, but can also be found on some chairs of the Windsor period. The splat is frequently pierced with decorative holes.

STYLE: Windsor and Queen Anne

PLACE: England

TIME: Early 1700s

BANISTER BACK CHAIR   A slat back chair with or without arms. The vertical slats may be lathe-turned, but are more likely to be flattened outlines of the banister turnings in a staircase handrail.

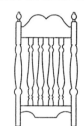

PLACE: Colonial America

TIME: 1700s

BARBER'S CHAIR   A modified corner chair. The barber's chair has an extended back rest to support the customer's head while he is being shaved. The extension was in the form of a longer center splat or a comb back. The chair in the illustration is of the Windsor style. Tastefully designed, the chair was not restricted to use in the barber shop. (See Corner Chair.)

STYLE: Windsor, Chippendale, and others

PLACE: England

TIME: 1700s

BARREL CHAIR   An upholstered chair with a curved back that resembles a barrel cut in half. (See Tub Chair.)

BENTWOOD CHAIR   A chair whose structural parts have been shaped under the effects of steam and pressure. It has one piece of bent wood making up the rear legs and back and a piece similarly formed to make the stretcher that reinforces the legs. The bentwood chair may have a cane or plywood seat. (See also Hoop Back, Loop Back, and Bow Back.)

PLACE: England and United States

TIME: Introduced in late 1800s

BERGERE CHAIR   An overstuffed armchair with upholstered back and sides. The term now is applied to any lightweight armchair as long as the back and sides are upholstered. More recently, the back and sides may even be caned instead of upholstered.

STYLE: Louis XIV

PLACE: Europe, particularly France

TIME: Late 1600s and mid-1700s

BOSTON ROCKER

A rocking chair, introduced in Boston, Massachusetts, having a form-fitting seat, slender spindles, a high back, and a top rail that is decorated with painted flowers.

PLACE: United States

TIME: Early 1800s

BOW BACK CHAIR

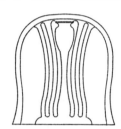

A chair in which the curved outer frame is continuous, having been bent into shape with heat and pressure. The bow is commonly found in the back of a Windsor chair. (See also Hoop Back Chair and Bentwood Chair.)

STYLE: Windsor

PLACE: England and United States

TIME: Early 1700s

BREWSTER CHAIR

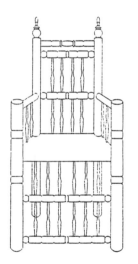

An armchair with heavy turned posts and double rows of turned spindles to form the sides and backrest. It has a wooden seat. The chair was the forerunner of the Carver Chair (see Carver Chair).

PLACE: Colonial New England

TIME: Early 1600s

CAPTAIN'S CHAIR

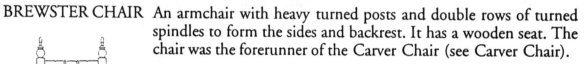

A low-backed armchair. The captain's chair got its name from its use on the pilot's deck of Mississippi steamboats.

STYLE: Windsor

PLACE: United States

TIME: Early 1800s

CAQUETEUSE A triangular seated chair with a tall, narrow back and curved outspreading arms. A woman's chair, the wide arms allowed for hoop dresses of the period. This chair is an outgrowth of the early back stool, which was no more than a stool with a narrow slat back. (Compare with Farthingale Chair.)

PLACE: France

TIME: 1500s

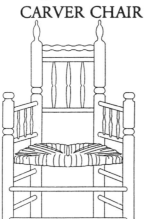

CARVER CHAIR A rush-seated chair of the pilgrim period. All four of the turned legs pass through the seat to be posts for the back of the chair and to support the arms. A single row of plain spindles makes up the arms, and the back is a single row of turned spindles. (Compare with Brewster Chair.)

PLACE: Colonial New England

TIME: 1600s

CHAIR BED A chair with an adjustable back rest and extendable foot rest so it can be made into a bed. The original was designed with side wings to support the head and was for sick persons so they could recline without first rising. Modern barber chairs and leather recliners are patterned on this style.

PLACE: Europe, particularly England

TIME: 1700s

CHAIR TABLE An armchair with a large round back, hinged so it can lower onto the arms. In the lowered position the circular back forms a table top.

PLACE: Europe, particularly England

TIME: Mid-1600s

CHAUFFEUSE A chair with a low seat and high back used to warm oneself at the fireplace.

PLACE: France

TIME: Early 1600s

COCK FIGHTING CHAIR   See Conversation Chair and Reading Chair.

CONVERSATION CHAIR   A unique chair whose striking feature is a padded rail designed to rise above seat level on the *front* of the chair and act as an armrest. Since the chair has no back, the gentleman sitting on the conversation chair straddles the seat, and leans forward to rest his arms on the padded rail. (See also Reading Chair.)

> STYLE: Sheraton
>
> PLACE: England
>
> TIME: Early 1800s

From left to right, Chair table, Chauffeuse, Conversation chair, Cricket

CORNER ARMCHAIR    An armchair with a round back or an angled back on two sides; the two backs will fit tight to the wall when placed in the corner of a room. The earliest corner chair was based on a triangle, having only three legs, later the chair took a diamond shape, with a fourth leg situated in the front.

> PLACE: England and United States
>
> TIME: Late 1600s to early 1800s

COURTING CHAIR    A style of corner chair with no arms and two backs, which are placed at right angles to fit into the corner of a room. The chair backs may suggest to your imagination the possibility of a milkmaid sitting on a farmer's lap, but the seat is entirely too small for two persons to sit side by side.

> PLACE: United States
>
> TIME: Early 1700s

CRICKET   An old English wooden footstool. The cricket has turned legs and is usually rather low.

PLACE: England

TIME: 1600s

CURRICLE   An armchair design based on an open two-wheel carriage.

STYLE: Sheraton

PLACE: England

TIME: Late 1700s

CURULE CHAIR   A folding chair or stool used by the ancient Romans. The legs of the curule chair were shaped like an "X".

PLACE: Rome

TIME: 100 A.D.

DANTE CHAIR   An "X"-shaped chair having four heavy legs curving up to arms with a leather seat. This is a Renaissance revival of the Roman Curule Chair (see Curule Chair). (See also Savonarola.)

PLACE: Italy

TIME: 1500s

DERBYSHIRE CHAIR   An English country chair. The backrest was made of two carved horizontal arched rails. The Derbyshire chair has the simple leg turnings that are typical of the Jacobean period. (See also Arcade Back Chair.)

PLACE: Derbyshire and Yorkshire districts of England

TIME: Early 1600s

DRAUGHT CHAIR   An easy chair with a high back and side wings. (See Wing Chair.)

EASY CHAIR   Any large, upholstered, cushioned lounge chair. The original easy chair was a wing chair of the early 18th century.

FANCY CHAIR   A chair that has been highly ornamented with paint. The chair is really somewhat plain compared to the complex carving found on other chairs of the same period. Indeed the only thing fancy is the paint job. Sheraton covered the natural wood grain with black paint and accentuated the chair's features with gold or colored pinstriping. The back splat, seat, and crest rail may also be decorated with stencilled fruit, leaves, or flower designs. (See also Boston Rocker and Hitchcock Chair.)

STYLE: Sheraton and others

PLACE: England and United States

TIME: Early 1800s

FARTHINGALE CHAIR A simple side chair with a broad seat and no arms. The farthingale chair was an ideal seat for women who wore the hoop skirts of the Elizabethan and Jacobean periods.

PLACE: England

TIME: Late 1500s and early 1600s

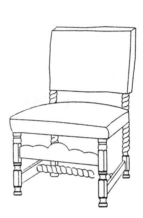

Left, Fancy chair; Right, Farthingale chair

FAUTEUIL An upholstered armchair with open sides. (Compare with Bergere Chair.)

PLACE: Europe, particularly France

TIME: Introduced in late 1600s

FIREHOUSE CHAIR A low back Windsor chair used extensively in volunteer firehouses. (See Captain's Chair and Smoker's Bow Chair.)

PLACE: United States

TIME: Early 1800s

GOSSIP'S CHAIR A chair with a broad seat to accommodate the hoop skirts of the 16th century. (See Caqueteuse.)

PLACE: France

TIME: 1500s

HALL CHAIR A formal chair placed in the hallway. The hall chair is not upholstered and not built for comfort, but is intended to receive messengers and other servants attired in coarse outdoor clothing. The back of the chair was often decorated with a carved crest and the owner's coat of arms.

PLACE: England

TIME: 1500s to 1700s

HITCHCOCK CHAIR A Fancy Chair (see Fancy Chair) painted to simulate rosewood. This popular side chair with straight turned front legs, Greek *klismos*-shaped rear legs (see Klismos), and a pillow back, was mass-produced in a factory run by Lambert Hitchcock in Hitchcocksville, Connecticut.

PLACE: United States

TIME: Early 1800s

HOGARTH CHAIR A Queen Anne chair (see Queen Anne Chair) that frequently appears in portraits and other illustrations by William Hogarth.

PLACE: England

TIME: Mid-1700s

HOOP BACK CHAIR A chair whose outer framing member is made of one continuous piece of bent wood. The hoop may even extend to the floor, providing rear legs for the chair. (Compare with Bentwood Chair and Bow Back Chair.)

PLACE: England and United States

TIME: 1700s

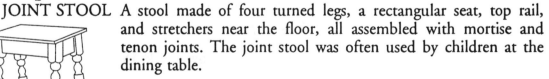

JOINT STOOL A stool made of four turned legs, a rectangular seat, top rail, and stretchers near the floor, all assembled with mortise and tenon joints. The joint stool was often used by children at the dining table.

PLACE: England

TIME: 1600s

KLISMOS A chair of classical Greece, with concave tapering legs, plaited seat, and an exaggerated curve in the back rest. The klismos was revived in the Regency period, late 18th and early 19th century A.D.

PLACE: Greece

TIME: 300 B.C.

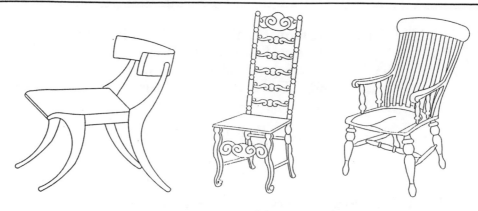

From left to right, Klismos, Ladder back chair, Lath back chair

LADDER BACK CHAIR
A chair whose backrest consists of a series of horizontal slats joined to the uprights. The backrest suggests the rungs of a ladder. The Slat Back Chair (see Slat Back Chair) was introduced as a piece of country furniture, and evolved to be the ladder back, a fashionable town chair.

PLACE: England and United States

TIME: 1700s

LATH BACK CHAIR
A chair of the Windsor period using thick vertical slats of wood, shaped to conform to a person's back, rather than the straight spindles that were typical for the back rest.

PLACE: England

TIME: Late 1800s

LATTICE BACK CHAIR
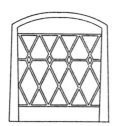
A chair with a backrest consisting of a delicate crisscrossing pattern of wood or metal. The lattice work is suggestive of the window tracery sometimes seen in the glass doors of cabinets and bookcases.

STYLE: Chippendale

PLACE: England

TIME: Mid-1700s

LOOP BACK CHAIR
A chair with an oval back. (See Bow Back Chair.)

LYRE BACK CHAIR
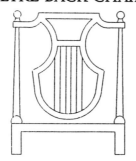
A chair with a back rest in the shape of a Greek lyre. Greek motifs have been very popular with major furniture designers and have been revived often. The illustration is of a chair back designed by Sheraton.

STYLE: Adam, Hepplewhite, Sheraton, Duncan Phyfe, others

PLACE AND TIME: France - 1650

England - early 1800s

United States - mid-1800s

MORRIS CHAIR   An upholstered armchair with adjustable back and removable cushions.

> STYLE: William Morris
>
> PLACE: United States
>
> TIME: Late 1800s

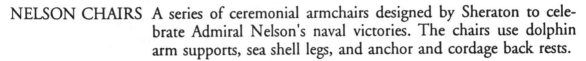

NELSON CHAIRS   A series of ceremonial armchairs designed by Sheraton to celebrate Admiral Nelson's naval victories. The chairs use dolphin arm supports, sea shell legs, and anchor and cordage back rests.

> PLACE: England
>
> TIME: Early 1800s

NIGHT STOOL   A bedroom chair containing a chamber pot. (See Close Chair.)

OTTOMAN   A low cushioned footstool.

PANEL BACK CHAIR   A heavy oak chair with a solid carved back. (See Wainscot Chair.)

> PLACE: Europe, particularly England
>
> TIME: 1500s

PERROQUET   A small armless chair suitable for use at a dining table. At a time when furniture was at a premium, the perroquet was conveniently moved from room to room by servants for extra seating as the need arose.

> PLACE: France
>
> TIME: 1600s

PLIANT   A folding stool for additional seating at the dining table.

> PLACE: France
>
> TIME: Early 1600s

QUAKER CHAIR   A bedroom chair with a round open back. The name for this chair is somewhat surprising as it was found in bedrooms of wealthy Victorians.

> PLACE: England and United States
>
> TIME: Mid-1800s

QUEEN ANNE CHAIR A chair having a single back splat, cut to resemble a vase, and cabriole legs—stylized representations of goat's legs. The Queen Anne chair may be straight-backed or with arms.

PLACE: England

TIME: Early 1700s

READING CHAIR A chair with arms and a small book stand mounted on what would ordinarily be the back. The reading chair was approached from the front and straddled. Resting his elbows on the arm rest, the gentleman was in a comfortable position to read anything placed on the book stand. (Compare with Conversation Chair.)

DESIGNER: Sheraton

PLACE: England

TIME: Introduced in 1808

ROCKING CHAIR A side chair mounted on two curved slats or runners. Almost any colonial chair could be made into a rocker, and consumers often made this conversion for themselves by notching the legs on existing chairs and fitting them to homemade rockers. A few of the factory-made styles became very popular. (See Boston Rocker and Salem Rocker.)

PLACE: United States

TIME: Late 1700s

SALEM ROCKER A popular rocking chair, similar to, though smaller than, the Boston Rocker (see Boston Rocker). The back is lower, but the Windsor-style spindle and the painted crest rail are the same.

PLACE: Salem, Massachusetts

TIME: 1800s

SAVONAROLA A folding chair based on the lines of the Roman Curule Chair (see Curule Chair).

PLACE: Italy

TIME: 1500s

SEDAN CHAIR A seat fitted with long horizontal poles, so it may be carried by two or four men. It is sometimes completely enclosed with curtained windows and a door on the front side. The sedan chair was popular with the religious leaders and royalty of 14th century Italy.

PLACE: Europe and Asia

TIME: 1200s

SGABELLO A chair made by simply adding a slab back to a stool. Although the design is basic, the carved decorations can be intricate, perhaps containing the coat of arms of its owner.

PLACE: Italy

TIME: 1400s

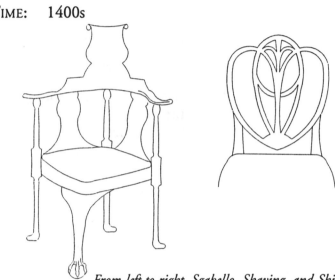

From left to right, Sgabello, Shaving, and Shield Back chairs

SHAVING CHAIR A corner chair with a high headrest. (See Barber's Chair.)

PLACE: England

TIME: Early 1700s

SHIELD BACK CHAIR A dining chair with a back in the shape of a shield. The shield pattern may be designed in a variety of motifs—ribbons, swagged fabric, feathers, or others.

STYLE: Hepplewhite

PLACE: England

TIME: Late 1700s

SIDE CHAIR Any chair without arms. Originally it was large and upholstered (see Farthingale). In modern usage it refers to a small chair without upholstery.

SLAT BACK CHAIR A chair with thin horizontal slats forming the back. The slat back is an early form of Ladder Back Chair (see Ladder Back Chair).

PLACE: Colonial America

TIME: Early 1600s

SLIPPER CHAIR   An upholstered dressing chair with short legs. It is of a convenient height for putting on slippers.

SMOKER'S BOW CHAIR   A low-backed armchair very similar to the Captain's Chair (see Captain's Chair) but popular in taverns and saloons.

STYLE: Windsor

PLACE: England and United States

TIME: Mid-1800s

SPINDLE BACK CHAIR   A simple side chair of the Windsor period. The legs, stretchers, and back are all made of lathe-turned spindles.

PLACE: England and United States

TIME: Early 1800s

SPOON BACK CHAIR   A side chair with contoured vertical back slats that conform to the shape of a person's body. The spoon back was a feature found in many Queen Anne Chairs (see Queen Anne Chair).

PLACE: England

TIME: Early 1700s

From left to right, Slat back chair, Smoker's bow chair, Spindle back chair, Spoon back chair, Tablet armchair

TABLET ARMCHAIR   An armchair with a small writing surface built onto the left arm.

STYLE: Windsor

PLACE: England and United States

TIME: Late 1700s

TUB CHAIR An upholstered easy chair with a sweeping round back rest that encompasses almost a half circle.

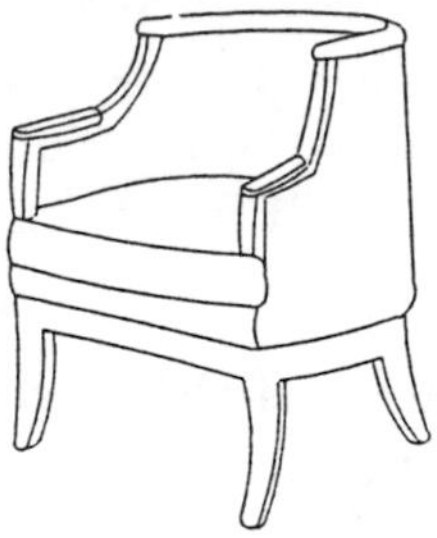

PLACE: France and England

TIME: Early 1800s

VASE SPLAT CHAIR A chair whose back is a wide vertical center splat in the shape of a vase.

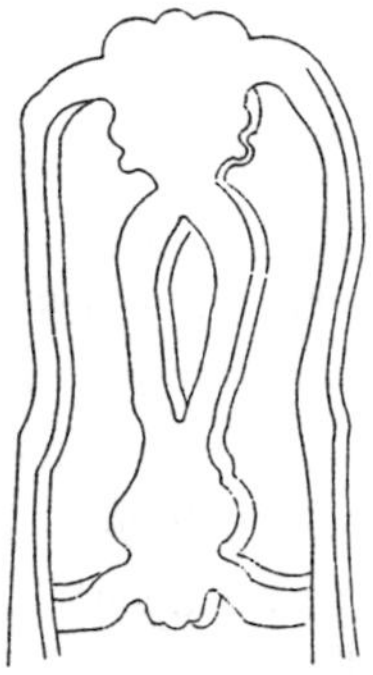

STYLE: Queen Anne

PLACE: England

TIME: Early 1700s

WAINSCOT CHAIR A panel-backed armchair. It is made of oak and heavily carved.

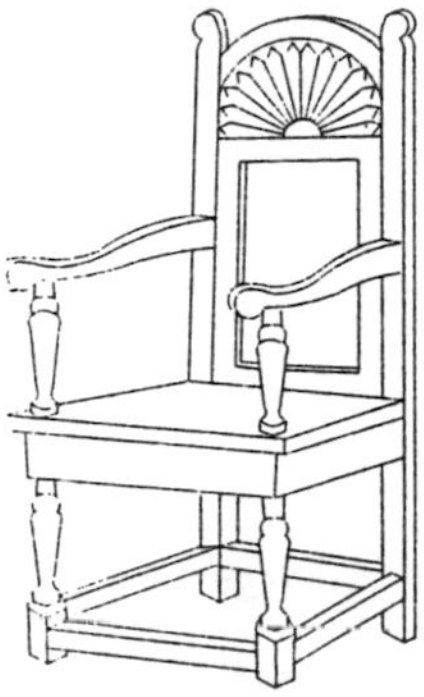

PLACE: France and England

TIME: 1500 to 1600

WHEEL BACK CHAIR A round or oval chair back with radiating spindles that resemble the spokes of a wheel.

STYLE: Hepplewhite

PLACE: England

TIME: Mid-1700s

WING CHAIR An overstuffed easy chair with a high back and projecting side wings to shield the user from drafts.

PLACE: England and United States

TIME: Introduced in 1700s

X-SHAPED CHAIR A chair whose legs are in the form of a letter "X". The Romans introduced the design in a folding stool called a Curule. A folding armchair based on this design, the Savonarola, was introduced in the Italian Renaissance. This same period produced the Dante, which follows the same design but will not fold. (See individual entries above.)

YORKSHIRE CHAIR A heavily carved side chair produced in the Yorkshire district of England. (See Derbyshire Chair and Arcade Back Chair.)

CHESTS

The chest has been an important item of furniture to people of all classes since the Middle Ages. Early householders wanted to store securely the few possessions they owned. When they could use a chest to sit on, or as a working surface, it was even more valuable. The chest was especially worthwhile to someone on the move—the nomad—and the pilgrim. No other piece of furniture had a place in the covered wagon, but if the pioneer owned two chests then two would go.

BOX STOOL A hinged-top square wooden chest of a height that makes a comfortable stool.

STYLE: Tudor

PLACE: England

TIME: 1500s

CASSAPANCA A long chest that has been converted to a settee by adding arms and a paneled back. The cassapanca is richly ornamented with wood carvings, but its square corners make it hard and uncomfortable.

SIZE: 6 feet long

PLACE: Italy

TIME: 1500s

CASSONI A chest with a hinged top. The cassoni is very highly decorated with linenfold and diaper panels, lace carvings, or intertwining tracery.

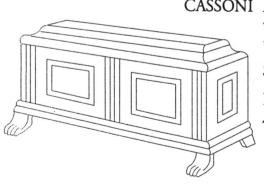

SIZE: 5 feet long

PLACE: Italy

TIME: 1400s

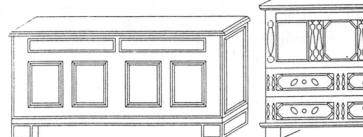

CEDAR CHEST   A storage chest made of fragrant cedar to protect woolens and furs against moths.

SIZE: 1½ to 3 feet long

PLACE: United States

TIME: Introduced in the late 1800s

From left to right, Coffer, Connecticut chest, Dower chest

COFFER   A chest, trunk, or strongbox used to store valuable articles. It is variously decorated, sometimes leather-covered and rather plain, and sometimes carved and highly ornamented. The coffer was one of Europe's earliest forms of furniture and could double as a chair or a table, depending on its size.

SIZE: 1½ to 4 feet long

PLACE: England

TIME: 1400s

CONNECTICUT CHEST   A hinge-top chest with drawers underneath. The feature that makes this chest different from the mule chest and others of its period is its decoration. The Connecticut chest has low relief carvings and raised knobs with split spindles of several sizes.

SIZE: 3 feet long

PLACE: New England

TIME: Late 1600s

DOWER CHEST   A marriage chest to store the clothes, household linens, and blankets that form a part of the prospective bride's dowry. The custom of preparing a dower chest was a practice common in all of Europe.

SIZE: 3½ feet long

PLACE: Europe

TIME: Late 1600s

DUG-OUT CHEST   A chest carved with an axe and an adze from a solid tree trunk. This most primitive form of chest or "trunk" was cut to a rectangular shape and fitted with a lid.

PLACE: Europe

TIME: 1200s

HADLEY CHEST   A dower chest distinguished by a pattern of tulip designs carved in low relief on the front and side panels.

PLACE: Hadley, Massachusetts

TIME: Late 1600s

HOPE CHEST   A dower chest (see Dower Chest) for the prospective bride to store the clothing, linens, and blankets that formed a part of her dowry. The term "hope chest" is more common to America.

MULE CHEST   A chest consisting of three compartments: two drawers below a shallow space accessible through a hinged lid. This transitional piece between the chest and the chest of drawers minimizes the problem of digging things from the bottom of a chest.

SIZE: 3 feet long

PLACE: England

TIME: Mid-1600s

NONESUCH CHEST   An Elizabethan chest decorated with architectural views made of inlaid colored woods. It was supposed that the scene represented Henry VIII's Palace of Nonesuch in Surrey, England.

PLACE: England

TIME: Late 1500s

TABLES AND DESKS

Crude heavy dining tables were introduced during the Dark Ages. Refectory tables of several sizes were used in the monasteries of Europe at this time.

The large dining table was both a necessity and a nuisance to the wealthy landowner of the 9th and 10th centuries. He recognized the convenience of the table while he was entertaining friends, but could not get over the fact that it took so much space when it lay idle. The trestle table, consisting of heavy planks bridged across two free-standing frames, answered the problem. The table was simply taken apart by servants and stored when it was not needed. This knock-down feature was also appreciated when the table was needed in another part of the castle.

The drawing rooms of the noblemen from the time of Queen Elizabeth, King James, King Charles of England, Louis XIII, and Louis XIV were remarkably free of clutter. Being sparsely furnished, there were not many flat storage places to keep an array of items necessary for comfortable living. Spectacles, keys, smoking and snuffing articles, watches, books, bags, and bells had to be carried or worn pinned or chained to a person's clothing rather than resting on a nearby table. Side tables and occasional tables did not become popular till the early 18th century.

AMBULANTES A small, easily portable table, used for serving tea, etc. The ambulantes is an early French version of an occasional table. (See Occasional Table.)

STYLE: Louis XV

PLACE: France

TIME: Mid-1700s

BEAU BRUMMELL A gentleman's dressing table with adjustable mirrors, candle brackets, shelves for cosmetics, and drawers for various toilet accessories. Such tables were in use by 18th century dandies, however, well before George Bryan Brummell was born.

STYLE: Georgian

PLACE: England

TIME: Mid-1700s

BUTTERFLY TABLE A drop-leaf table whose leaves are supported by a solid swinging bracket. The name comes from the shape of the table when the supports are extended open.

PLACE: England and United States

TIME: Late 1600s

CANTERBURY A side stand with vertical divisions originally intended to hold sheet music or books when not otherwise in use. Sheraton suggested that it be used at the dining table and designed in a deep partitioned semicircular shelf to carry a supper tray and plates. (Compare with Dumb Waiter.)

STYLE: Sheraton and others

PLACE: England

TIME: Late 1700s

CARD TABLE A folding table for playing cards. The folding legs have remained a typical feature, although some gaming tables have had finely ornamented permanent "S" curved legs ending in a ball and claw foot. (See Game Table.)

STYLE: Carolean

PLACE: Europe

TIME: Late 1600s

CARLTON TABLE A writing desk flanked by a bank of small drawers and compartments to hold writing materials and letters.

PLACE: England

TIME: Late 1700s

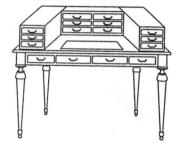

COASTER An early form of lazy Susan, this small round tray is mounted on wheels so it can be moved about on a dining table to serve food and drink.

PLACE: England

TIME: 1700s

CONCERTINA TABLE A card or game table that expands to twice its size as the ends pull apart and hinged side frames open. The table top is made of two sections joined with hinges. When the concertina is folded closed, the top is double thickness; when in use, the hinged top opens and is supported by the expanded frame.

PLACE: England

TIME: Mid to late 1700s

CONSOLE TABLE A shallow table designed to fit against a wall. The console table was originally attached to the wall and was supported solely by brackets. The name came to describe all shallow tables when one side was secured to a wall even if the other side had two legs extending to the floor. (See Pier Table.)

PLACE: England and France

TIME: 1600s to early 1800s

COUNTER A long board or table behind which a seller stands and on which goods are displayed. It has been suggested that the counter received its name from a medieval table where the landlord sat to receive payments from his tenants. (See Rent Table.)

CREDENCE A table used in the Middle Ages to prepare food before it was served. One theory suggests that the name came from the practice of tasting the food at this table, testing it for the presence of poison before serving to guests. The credence evolved into the buffet-sideboard and cupboard.

PLACE: Italy

TIME: 1200s

CRICKET TABLE A small, round three-legged table.

STYLE: Jacobean

PLACE: England

TIME: Early 1600s

DAVENPORT A small kneehole writing desk with slope-top writing surface and drawers that are accessible from one side.

SIZE: 2 feet wide

PLACE: England

TIME: Early 1800s

DESK Any writing table equipped with drawers, compartments, and a space for writing, drawing, and reading. The original desk was a lap box with a sloping lid hinged to open.

DRAW TABLE A table with a pair of draw leaves that are hidden under the table top. When the leaves are drawn to the open position the table is almost double its original length.

STYLE: Elizabethan

PLACE: England

TIME: Late 1500s

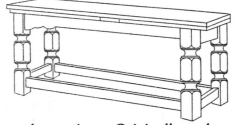

DRESSER The term has had several meanings. Originally a dresser was a medieval kitchen or dining room table on which meats or other foods were prepared before serving. In the 17th century the dresser acquired shelves and drawers primarily for storing and displaying eating utensils. (See Credence.) Today, it refers to a dressing table or commode with drawers for storing clothing and outfitted with a tilting mirror.

DRESSING TABLE   A table equipped with drawers and a mirror for applying cosmetics, etc. The extent of its elaboration depends on whether it was designed for ladies or gentlemen. (See Beau Brummell and Poudreuse.)

DROP-LEAF TABLE   A table with hinged leaves that can be lowered to the side when not in use. (See Gate Leg Table, Pembroke Table, and Butterfly Table.)

DRUM TABLE   A round table with a deep apron containing drawers.

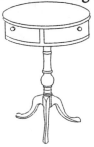

PLACE: England

TIME: Late 1700s

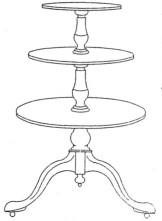

DUMB WAITER   A round serving stand on wheels placed near the hostess's end of a dining table to hold additional food, plates, and utensils. The stand consists of two to four trays mounted one above the other on a central post.

PLACE: France and England

TIME: Early 1700s

EAGLE TABLE   A console table supported by the head and outspread wings of an eagle. The eagle's head, wings, and claws have been used to decorate furniture for centuries, finding revival in the Renaissance, the Empire period, and in post-Revolutionary America.

STYLE: Baroque

PLACE: Italy and France

TIME: Early 1700s

ESCRITOIRE   A drop-front writing desk. The escritoire is smaller than its English cousin, the Secretary (see Secretary).

PLACE: France

TIME: Late 1600s

FALL-LEAF TABLE   A table with hinged leaves that can fold open to make a larger work surface. (See Gate Leg Table.)

GAME TABLE A specialized table for playing cards and other games. The table top may be inlaid with a game board for playing chess or backgammon. Game tables have been in use since the 16th century. The foldover table top in the illustration was developed during the early 1700s.

PLACE: Europe

TIME: 1500s to 1800s

GATE-LEG TABLE A drop-leaf table with hinged supports or "gates." In the open position, the gate swings open and the table top rests on it.

PLACE: England

TIME: 1600s

From left to right, Gate-leg table, Kidney table, Loo table

HARLEQUIN TABLE A deep-aproned table that houses a mechanism raising an array of drawers or pigeonholes when the top is opened. The harlequin mechanism is used variously as a tea table, liquor cabinet, writing table, or dressing table.

STYLE: Sheraton

PLACE: England

TIME: Late 1700s

KIDNEY TABLE Any table whose top is kidney-shaped to allow the user to sit in the concave curve. The kidney table may serve as a writing table, dressing table, or commode.

PLACE: England and France

TIME: Mid-1700s

KNEEHOLE DESK A desk or bureau with a bank of drawers on both sides and a central open space for the user's legs, allowing him to draw very near the table top.

PLACE: Introduced in Europe

TIME: Introduced in the 1700s

KNOCK-DOWN FURNITURE A piece of furniture that easily folds or comes apart and stores flat for shipping. A card table with folding legs is a modern example of knock-down furniture.

PLACE: Europe

TIME: 1400s

LAZY SUSAN A revolving food tray that sits in the center of the dining table. It can be reached by anyone at the table and minimizes passing and reaching.

PLACE: United States

TIME: Introduced in the late 1700s

LOO TABLE An oval or round game table of the Victorian period for playing a card game called "Lanterloo." The loo table had a hinged top that could be folded up, reducing the amount of floor space it occupied and displaying the patterned decorations crafted into the playing surface.

PLACE: England

TIME: Late 1800s

NESTED TABLES A set of three or four small tables, graduated in size. Each table fits inside the next largest to conserve space when the set is not in use. Sheraton designed them in sets of three and four.

PLACE: Introduced in England

TIME: Introduced in the 1800s

NIGHT TABLE A bedside table. The table sometimes contains a deep drawer that can be pulled open to reveal a wash stand or a chamber pot.

PLACE: Europe and United States

TIME: Early 1800s

OCCASIONAL TABLE Any small, easily moved side table. The occasional table may serve as tea table, end table, lamp table, game table, or whatever the occasion requires.

> PLACE: Europe and United States

> TIME: Introduced in the 1600s

PEDESTAL DESK A writing desk consisting of a writing surface supported by two pedestals of drawers. The space between the pedestals allows room for the user's knees. (See Kneehole Desk.)

> TIME: Introduced in the 1700s

PEDESTAL TABLE A round or oval dining table supported by a central column with four spreading feet (sometimes ball and claw feet). The pedestal table is a revival of a style that originated in ancient Rome where it was made of bronze.

> PLACE: England

> TIME: Late 1700s

PEMBROKE TABLE A lightweight occasional table with two short drop leaves. It may have one or two shallow drawers in the apron. (See Sofa Table.)

> STYLE: Sheraton, Chippendale, and Duncan Phyfe

> PLACE: England and United States

> TIME: Late 1700s and early 1800s

PIE CRUST TABLE A round tea table with a scalloped edge recalling the edges of a homemade pie crust. The top is usually attached to a central post mounted on tripod legs. Sometimes the top is tippable so it can be stored tight to a wall when the table is not in use.

> STYLE: Chippendale and Sheraton

> PLACE: England and United States

> TIME: Mid to late 1700s

PIER TABLE A shallow console table designed to sit tight against a wall. The pier table holds an urn or a vase of flowers and is intended for decoration rather than a practical work surface. The table is frequently surmounted by a pier glass and may be flanked by elaborate wall sconces. The pier table-pier glass combination was very popular in wealthy households.

STYLE: Chippendale, Hepplewhite, Sheraton, and Adam

PLACE: France and England

TIME: Mid-1700s

POUDREUSE A lady's dressing table popular during the reign of King Louis XV. Sliding tops and hinged mirrors are prominent features of this powder table. The poudreuse served the French lady as the Beau Brummell (see Beau Brummell) served the English gentleman.

PLACE: France

TIME: Mid-1700s

REFECTORY TABLE A long, narrow table such as may have been used in a monastery dining room of the Middle Ages. Some refectory tables can serve as many as twenty persons, others as few as six. (See also Trestle Table.)

PLACE: Europe

TIME: 900 A.D.

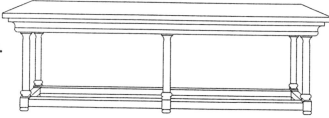

RENT TABLE A round or octagonal table with drawers around the apron. An early counter. The drawers of the rent table were marked with the days of the week and were used as a filing system by the landlord.

PLACE: England

TIME: 1500s

ROLL-TOP DESK A desk with a flexible pull-down lid. The roll-top is made of thin strips of wood, hinged as a result of being glued to a canvas backing.

PLACE AND TIME: Introduced in France - late 1600s

United States - 1800s to the present

SECRETARY A fall-front writing desk that is topped with a small set of book shelves.

PLACE: England, France, and United States

TIME: Late 1600s to late 1800s

SEWING TABLE A small work table with drawers and a folding lid, which covers the table when it is not in use. With the lid open an 18-inch hole cut into the center of the table is exposed. A pouch is mounted under the hole to catch the needlework and keep it clean. The sewing table was a standard item in most homes till the sewing machine replaced it.

STYLE: Sheraton, Hepplewhite, Duncan Phyfe

PLACE: England, France, Germany, and United States

TIME: Late 1700s to 1850

SLANT-FRONT DESK Any desk or secretary with an inclining lid that hides the writing materials, small drawers, pigeon holes, etc. The slanted front evolved from the early custom of reading or writing on sloped surfaces.

SOFA TABLE A Pembroke table placed next to a sofa. Most tables were 30 inches high; the sofa table was 2 to 3 inches shorter. It was used for reading, writing, playing games, or holding items needed by an invalid.

STYLE: Georgian

PLACE: England

TIME: Early 1800s

STAND   Any small table whose purpose is to hold or display a specific article: lamp stand, candle stand, music stand, plant stand, urn stand, wig stand, etc.

TAVERN TABLE   A rugged table with simple lathe-turned legs. The table is large enough to serve two persons comfortably yet small enough to be moved easily from place to place in the tavern.

PLACE: United States

TIME: Mid-1700s

TEA TABLE   A table just large enough to hold a tea service. Tea was introduced to England in the early 1700s and was soon very popular. The small, round tripod table became a part of the tea-drinking ritual.

PLACE: England

TIME: Mid-1700s

TILT-TOP TABLE   A table whose top is hinged to its pedestal base and may be tilted vertically either to store the table tightly against a wall or to display a particularly fine example of wood grain or inlaid decoration. (See also Loo Table and Pie Crust Table.)

TRESTLE TABLE   A heavy table originally made of loose boards laid on folding supports called trestles. The trestle table was used primarily for dining in the Middle Ages. The table top became a solid slab in the late 15th century but remained free of the base so it could be easily removed and stored when the hall was needed for some activity other than dining. In the late 16th century, the knock-down feature was abandoned, and most tables were firmly attached to their trestles.

PLACE: Europe

TIME: 900s to mid-1600s

VANITY   A Dressing Table (see Dressing Table).

FURNITURE STYLES

ADAM   Architect Robert Adam and two of his brothers, William and James, developed furniture with a classical motif to accompany the rooms he designed. The rooms have a strong vertical line that is emphasized by the delicate tapering legs of the furniture. The tables are generally long and narrow, designed to fit a specific space on a wall. Some of the furniture was painted white to go with the space, which was typically very bright. With his brothers, Robert Adam produced both the furniture and the rooms from 1758 to 1790.

PLACE: England

TIME: 1758 to 1790

ART NOUVEAU   A style of design characterized by sinuous, undulating lines involving plant forms and exotic coloring.

PLACE AND TIME: Introduced in France and England - 1880s

Spread to Italy and Germany - 1890

Brought to the United States in 1900

Style fell out of favor in 1920

BAROQUE   A style encompassing many art forms: architecture, painting, sculpture, music, and furniture. Baroque furniture is often heavy and very busy with swirling lines of carved scrolls, shells, and flowers. Complex carvings whirl in thick crusts of ornament. Human and animal forms and cupids are prominent motifs in the elaborate decoration.

PLACE: Italy

TIME: Mid-1500s to early 1700s

BIEDERMEIER   A style of furniture design—essentially a heavy, stolid variation of French Empire.

PLACE: Germany

TIME: 1800 to 1850

CAROLEAN   Pertaining to styles in vogue during the reigns of King Charles I and II of England. The Restoration period coincides with the reign of Charles II. The furniture of this period in England follows the rectilinear tradition of the Middle Ages, and resists most of the extravagance of baroque. The process of inlaying was borrowed, however, and table surfaces are rich in geometric patterns of inlaid wood grains.

PLACE: England

TIME: 1625 to 1685

CHIPPENDALE Furniture designer Thomas Chippendale was an adapter who combined rococo and gothic motifs with a Chinese influence. His dining room chair is perhaps most easily recognized, having an upholstered seat, pierced back splat, and cabriole legs (stylized goat leg) with leaf carvings near the top and ending with a ball and claw foot.

PLACE: England

TIME: 1750 to 1790

DIRECTOIRE A style that revived the furniture forms of classical Greece and Rome, combining these lines with Louis XVI motifs. This style was prevalent in the period immediately following the French Revolution.

PLACE: France

TIME: 1790 to 1804

DUNCAN PHYFE Scottish-born American cabinet maker and furniture designer Duncan Phyfe produced furniture strongly influenced by contemporary classical styles that were current at his time—Directoire, Regency, and Empire. Phyfe had favorite figures that recurred often in his works, such as the lyre motif that appeared in chair backs and table supports and the slender animal chair legs terminating in a small foot called a "dog" or "rat-paw."

PLACE: New York

TIME: 1780s to 1820s

ELIZABETHAN Pertaining to styles in vogue during the reign of Queen Elizabeth I of England. The furniture of this period was made of thick slabs of oak or walnut and was decorated with gothic arches and carved geometric patterns. Bulbous turnings resembling melons were prominent on table legs and bed posts.

PLACE: England

TIME: 1533 to 1603

FRENCH EMPIRE A style of furniture growing from the Directoire period (see Directoire). Greek, Roman, and Egyptian motifs continued to be dominant.

PLACE: France

TIME: 1804 to 1815

FRENCH PROVINCIAL A style of furniture popular in the countryside of France. Although the furniture belongs to the rural areas, it is not crude and rustic, nor is it like the grand pieces found in the palaces of the king and his noblemen. It has a sophistication of its own.

PLACE: France

TIME: Late 1600s to early 1800s

GEORGIAN   Pertaining to styles in vogue during the reigns of the first four Georges of England. This period saw the rise of the great English furniture designers, Chippendale, Hepplewhite, Adam, and Sheraton (see individual entries).

PLACE: England

TIME: 1714 to 1830

HEPPLEWHITE   Furniture designer George Hepplewhite produced elegant furniture with slender tapering legs. The shield back chair was a favorite motif. The designs he sketched for *The Cabinetmaker and Upholsterer's Guide* published in 1788 influenced designers who immediately followed him.

PLACE: London, England

TIME: 1760s to 1780s

JACOBEAN   Pertaining to the styles in vogue during the reign of James I of England. The furniture of this period consisted of a lighter, simpler version of the Renaissance style, which was late in coming to England. Cupboards, tables, and chests are still carved and rectilinear, but the carvings are more delicate, and smaller diameter turned legs replace the heavier bulb turnings on tables and bedposts. There is an increased use of upholstery.

PLACE: England

TIME: 1603 to 1625

LOUIS XIV   Pertaining to styles in vogue during the reign of King Louis XIV of France. The furniture style is a modified form of baroque using black woods, appliqués of gold leaf, and inlays of marble, shells, or ivory.

PLACE: France

TIME: 1643 to 1715

LOUIS XV   Pertaining to styles in vogue during the reign of King Louis XV of France. Furniture is sculpted with curved lines, rounded edges, and lacy flat carvings. The period coincides with the rococo (see Rococo).

PLACE: France

TIME: 1715 to 1774

LOUIS XVI   Pertaining to styles in vogue during the reign of King Louis XVI of France. The prevailing rococo style is greatly refined. The curves of tabletops, chest fronts, and chair legs are straightened.

PLACE: France

TIME: 1774 to 1793

QUEEN ANNE An English furniture style that coincides with the period of Queen Anne's reign. The most remembered piece of furniture from this period is the Queen Anne chair having a single baluster splat in the back and "S"-shaped legs.

PLACE: England

TIME: 1702 to 1714

REGENCY A period of furniture design that parallels the time when George Prince of Wales acted as Regent of England. The furniture of this period was influenced by another revival in classical motifs — Greek *klismos* saber legs and "X"-form bases to support chairs, and animal and human figures to support tables.

PLACE: England

TIME: 1793 to 1820

RENAISSANCE The period of the revival of arts and letters. The furniture was decorated with carvings, gothic arches, and tracery following the lines set in the architecture of the period.

PLACE: Beginning in Italy and spreading to all of Europe

TIME: Early 1400s to late 1500s

RESTORATION The English Restoration coincides with the monarchy of Charles II, and is sometimes called Carolean (see Carolean). English furniture of this period begins to use some curved lines in the designs, but it never approaches the extravagance of baroque, current in other European contries. The daybed is introduced at this time, and caning is much used in place of solid wood surfaces.

PLACE: England

TIME: 1660 to 1688

ROCOCO A style encompassing many art forms. It is a modified form of baroque (see Baroque). In furniture, the style is characterized by elaborate and profuse carved ornamentation simulating flowers, foliage, shells, and scrolls. Square corners and straight lines are rejected in favor of curves and rounded corners.

PLACE AND TIME: France - 1720 to 1800

Western Europe - 1780

SHERATON Furniture designer Thomas Sheraton was well known for the drawings and discussions that were published in several books. He designed all forms of furniture but is best remembered for his chair designs.

PLACE: England

TIME: 1790 to early 1800s

TUDOR A period of style covering the rule of the English Tudor kings.

The important rulers of this time were King Henry VIII and Elizabeth I. The furniture of this period is rectangular and heavy, made of oak, and follows the lines of contemporary architecture with gothic arches and carved tracery.

PLACE: England

TIME: 1485 to 1603

VICTORIAN Pertaining to styles in vogue from 1837 to 1901 during the reign of Queen Victoria of England. This is a period of revivals in furniture. Louis XV motifs and those of the Greek and Gothic styles were revisited. Victorian upholsterers also revived a style of tufting used in the Turkish ottoman.

PLACE: England and United States

TIME: 1837 to 1901

WILLIAM AND MARY A furniture style in vogue during the reigns of King William III and Queen Mary of England. The pieces of this period are less bulky than the Elizabethan and Jacobean furniture that preceded it, having slender balusters and trumpet-turned legs on the tables and chairs.

PLACE: England

TIME: 1650 to 1702

WILLIAM MORRIS William Morris promoted the Arts and Crafts Movement in furniture design. He is famous as the manufacturer of an adjustable lounge chair.

PLACE: England

TIME: Mid to late 1800s

WINDSOR A chair style consisting of turned legs, bow backs, and straight spindles, which originated in rural England in the early 18th century.

PLACE: England and United States

TIME: Early 1700s to late 1900s

Clocks and Watches

---TIMEKEEPING---

A clock is an instrument for measuring periods of time and indicating the hours and minutes as they elapse. At first this information was reported as a bell tolled. Later the hour was told as hands moved over a clock face.

The first public clock was a medieval watchtower housing an hour glass, a bell, and a man. As soon as the sand glass emptied, the man announced the hour with a stroke on the bell. In the 12th century a mechanical clock replaced the hour glass, but not the man. The hourly ringing of the bell became a mechanical operation a hundred years later, but the watchman still could not go home, as the clock needed constant attention to keep the mechanism running at a uniform rate. Accurate, reliable clocks were placed in cathedral towers in the mid-1300s. Even these continued the tradition of keeping track of hourly blocks of time. For three hundred years this was enough—one hand was sufficient. The minute hand was not added to the clock face until 1670.

BANJO CLOCK A weight-driven pendulum clock, shaped somewhat like a banjo. This clock was mass-produced in the 1800s for use in homes and businesses. It was especially popular with railway companies and was featured in many train stations.

SIZE: 32 to 44 inches high

PLACE: United States

TIME: Patented in 1802

BLACK FOREST CLOCK A clock whose workings are made entirely of hardwood. The gears are hand-carved from beech or boxwood. Despite immediate popularity, clock-making in this area did not develop fully till the mid-1700s.

SIZE: 9 to 12 inches high

PLACE: Black Forest, Germany and Switzerland

TIME: 1680 to 1800

BOX CHRONOMETER   A seagoing chronometer mounted on gimbals so it will remain level. (See Marine Chronometer.)

BRACKET CLOCK   A weight-driven clock that stands on a wall bracket, a mantel, or a table. (See Lantern Clock.)

CANDLE CLOCK   A candle marked with bands to indicate the passage of time as the candle burns. This timer dates from medieval times. Some say it was invented by King Arthur. A similar device was developed in the 18th century, measuring the supply of fuel that remained in a whale oil lamp as it burned. (See Whale Oil Timer.)

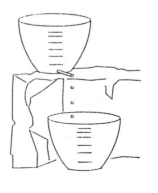

SIZE: 6 to 8 inches high

PLACE: Europe, particularly England

TIME: 500s

CHATELAINE WATCH   A watch that can be carried on a chain attached to the waist band. The chatelaine watch joined the other necessary items carried by a noble lady: mirror, purse, keys, etc.

SIZE: 3 inches in diameter

PLACE: Europe

TIME: 1600s to late 1700s

CHRONOMETER   A clock, used in navigation, that measures time very accurately. The chronometer is used on board ships to determine longitude.

PLACE: Introduced in England

TIME: Introduced in the 1700s

CLEPSYDRA   Any timekeeping device that involves water dripping from a container. One model is a bucket of water with a small hole drilled near its bottom. The water drips out slowly, and the water level is calibrated to show the passage of time.

Another type has a dish with a hole drilled in its bottom, floating in a pool of water. The dish slowly fills with water and finally sinks. This event marks one unit of time.

PLACE AND TIME: First introduced in Egypt in 1400 B.C.

Refined to keep reliable time in Greece and Rome in 100 to 400 A.D.

Water clocks spread into Europe where they remained in use till 1350 A.D.

CLOCK FACES

All clock faces were originally marked with Roman numerals to identify the hours. These predominated until the late 19th century, when Arabic numerals began to be popular because they were more familiar and easier to read. Roman numerals had a good aesthetic look as they appeared on the dial. The numeral IIII was retained even after IV came into vogue for this very reason—it balanced the VIII and looked better.

PLACE: Europe and United States

TIME: 1350 to the late 1800s

COFFIN CLOCK

A 17th-century common name for a pendulum clock housed in a long case. (See Long Case Clock.)

CUCKOO CLOCK

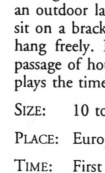

A clock with a wooden cuckoo bird that pops out of a door and signals the hour with a series of chirps. The cuckoo clock with a wooden movement was made in the Black Forest region.

SIZE: 8 to 14 inches high

PLACE: Switzerland and Germany

TIME: 1730 to the present

GRANDFATHER CLOCK

Another name for a Long Case Clock. The name comes from the song "My Grandfather's Clock" by Henry Clay Work, written in 1876. (See Long Case Clock.)

HOUR GLASS

A sand glass designed to measure intervals of one hour. (See Sand Glass.)

LANTERN CLOCK

A weight-driven clock deriving its name from its resemblance to an outdoor lantern of the same period. The lantern clock must sit on a bracket (or hang on a wall) in order for the weights to hang freely. Lantern clocks are primarily concerned with the passage of hours and have only one hand. The single hand displays the time visually and a bell chimes on the hour.

SIZE: 10 to 12 inches high

PLACE: Europe, particularly England

TIME: First built in the early 1600s; common in 1658

LONG CASE CLOCK A clock housed in a long upright case at least six feet tall. The long case is necessary to house a 5-foot pendulum. A mechanism is included in the roomy framework that is capable of chiming fifteen-minute intervals and of playing a short tune on the hour. It is a beautifully crafted item of furniture and became a tremendously popular household clock as soon as it was introduced. The nickname "coffin clock" was attached to it at an early date; the term "grandfather clock" came in 1876.

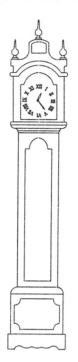

SIZE: 6 to 8 feet high

PLACE: Europe, especially England

TIME: 1660 to the present

Widely available by the early 1700s

MAINSPRING A coiled flat spring to power gear-driven mechanisms, including the clock or watch. The mainspring was a big step forward in clock-making. It allowed miniaturization and portability.

PLACE: Germany

TIME: 1500

MANTEL CLOCK A clock designed to sit on a fireplace mantel. The term was first applied, during the time of Louis XVI, to a style of clock highly decorated with figures, animals, and cupids. Later it applied to any clock that commanded the mantel's space.

SIZE: 2 feet wide by 1½ feet high

PLACE: Introduced in France

TIME: Introduced in the late 1700s

MARINE CHRONOMETER A clock used at sea to determine longitude. The chronometer is mounted on gimbals to minimize the effects of the ship's motion on the clockworks.

POCKET WATCH Any watch designed to be carried in a man's waistcoat pocket. The first pocket watches had only one hand and were highly decorated, the case being much more important than the accuracy of the mechanism. Even though most of the first portable clocks were small enough to be carried in the pocket, it didn't happen. Watches were a bit too large and awkward, pockets were not overly plentiful, and the vogue of pulling the watch from a hiding place had not yet become fashionable. Watches were placed on tables, fastened to the clothing, or hung around the neck on a chain. Glass was added to protect the hand in 1610.

SIZE: 2½ inches in diameter, 1 inch thick

PLACE: Introduced in Europe

TIME: Early 1600s

SAND GLASS   A dry form of water clock consisting of sand trickling through a glass globe with a narrow waist. Two such glass globes are sealed end to end and housed in an open wooden frame. The top globe is filled with dry sand (or powdered eggshells). The emptying time is controlled to a specific period of time, and the unit is thus named a "three-minute timer" or an "hour glass." The sand glass evolved, and the convenience, accuracy, and beauty of the unit were greatly improved. The popularity of the sand glass for measuring short periods of time continued into the 16th century.

SIZE: Size varies widely according to application; 4 to 12 inches high

PLACE: Europe and Asia

TIME: 100 A.D. to 1500s

SUNDIAL   An instrument that indicates time by casting the shadow of a rod on a numbered dial.

SIZE: Varies from pocket size to a European model that was mounted high on the face of a building

PLACE AND TIME: Babylonia - 2000 B.C.

Egypt - 800 B.C.

Greece - 500 B.C.

Rome - 300 B.C.

Europe - 100 A.D. to 1500s

WATCH   A spring-driven timepiece miniaturized and capable of being carried. (See Pocket Watch and Chatelaine Watch.)

SIZE: 2 to 3 inches in diameter, 1½ inches thick

PLACE: Europe, particularly Germany, France, the Netherlands

TIME: Introduced in the late 1500s

WHALE OIL TIMER   A whale oil lamp equipped with a gauge that reads the rate of oil consumption.

SIZE: 10 inches high

PLACE: United States

TIME: Introduced in 1780

WRISTWATCH A watch worn on a strap or band that fits around a wrist. Women of the courts of Europe were wearing wristwatches as a novelty in the 18th century. Men shunned them as being effeminate till soldiers of the First World War proved their practicality. The earliest wristwatch was nothing more than a small pocket watch fitted to a wide band.

SIZE: 1¼ to 2¼ inches in diameter

PLACE: Europe and United States

TIME: 1910 to the present

Brief History of Timekeeping	
Egyptians develop the clepsydra (water clock)	1400 B.C.
Egyptians produce a sundial with six time divisions	800 B.C.
Greeks and Chinese use sundials	500 B.C.
Clepsydra is introduced to Rome	157 B.C.
Sandglass timer is developed	100 A.D.
Chinese build a water-driven mechanical clock	1090
Italians have a faceless tower clock that chimes the hour	1335
Weight-driven clock mechanism is developed	1350
French install a mechanical clock in a tower	1350
European homes have household clocks	1400
Mainspring is invented by Peter Henlein, German locksmith	1500
Peter Henlein invents a portable clock	1500
"Nuremberg egg," the first spherical watch, is produced	1502
Pocket watch is available	1600
Pendulum is introduced as a regulating device	mid-1600s
Long case (grandfather's) clock is developed	1660
English include a minute hand on the clock face	1680
Ladies wear miniaturized watches as a brooch	1700
Second hand is added to the clock face	1770
Factory-made watch is available	1855
Wristwatch becomes popular	1910
Timex introduces inexpensive durable wristwatch	1949
Battery-operated wristwatch is produced	1957

Lamps and Lanterns

— EARLY LAMPS —

History's first lamps were simply a burning wick of moss or plant fiber floating in a bath of animal grease. Terra cotta lamps and candles made of animal fats were in constant use from the times of Babylonia and ancient Egypt to the end of the American Civil War. Thousands of years passed without any appreciable change in this technology. Discoveries of new fuels and inventions of light-producing devices finally began in the middle of the 18th century. Once started, these long overdue discoveries grew, continuing unabated for two and a half centuries to the present day. Each new step—from the improved oil lamp, to gas, to electricity—has brought us brighter, safer, cleaner light.

An early oil lamp consists of a terra cotta bowl to hold the oil, with a spout to hold a wick. The fuel burns with a dim yellow light and produces an uncomfortable amount of smoke.

SIZE: Bowl - 4 inches in diameter

PLACE: Babylonia and ancient Egypt

TIME: 3000 B.C.

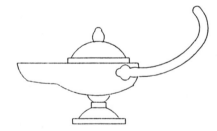

One of the first uses of bronze was in the manufacture of oil lamps. The lamp, made of metal, was more expensive, but it was exactly like the pottery lamp in operation. It has a spout on one end that holds the wick, a handle on the other end, and the body acts as a fount to hold the oil.

SIZE: 8 to 12 inches long

PLACE: Mid-East, especially Arabia

TIME: 1800 B.C.

ALADDIN'S LAMP This lamp is named from an ancient collection of stories called *The Thousand and One Nights.*

SIZE: 8 to 12 inches long

PLACE: Ancient Arabia, India, and Persia

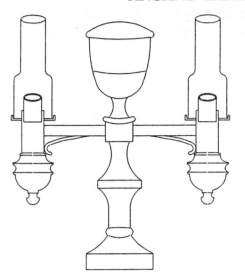

ARGAND LAMP   A revolutionary lamp design having a circular arrangement for the wick accompanied by a central draft burner. This wick design allowed oxygen to reach all parts of the wick, greatly increasing burning efficiency.

The Argand lamp produced a much brighter light and greatly reduced smoke. The first glass chimney was invented almost immediately and was also produced by the laboratories of Ami Argand. These improvements provided a major breakthrough in lamp design, the first in literally thousands of years.

SIZE: 1½ feet high

PLACE: Invented in Switzerland, immediately spread to all of Europe

TIME: 1784 to the early 1900s

ASTRAL LAMP   A lamp design said to be an improvment over the Argand lamp, producing less shadow. This lamp has its oil supply housed in a circular tube (like a bicycle tire). The reservoir surrounds the rim of the lamp and uses gravity to feed the wick through small pipes.

SIZE: 14 inches high, 10 inches in diameter

PLACE: Europe, Australia, and United States

TIME: Introduced in 1820

BETTY LAMP   An oil lamp with a covered reservoir and a hole in the body to hold the wick secure. Because the oil is enclosed and spillage retarded, the Betty lamp is safer and cleaner than the Crusie and the Phoebe (see Crusic and Phoebe). This lamp demonstrates the tinsmith's ability to duplicate the pottery lamp in use since primitive times. The Betty lamp always comes with a sharply pointed rod chained to the body. This pick is used to renew the wick when it burns away, by catching at a new section of rag.

The hanging spur for the lamp is characteristic of all open-dish oil burners. The hook can be attached to a peg, chair back, or any handy protrusion. The sharp awl point on the end of the spur can be driven into a wooden post or forced into the cracks between boards or rocks in a home's construction.

SIZE: 8 to 12 inches long

PLACE: Colonial America

TIME: 1600 to 1850

BULL'S EYE LANTERN

A whale oil lantern fitted with a lens. This lantern was used extensively on board ships, in gold mines, on railroads, and by watchmen. A kerosene version of the bull's eye lamp was introduced in the 1860s.

SIZE: 10 to 12 inches high

PLACE: Europe and United States

TIME: 1790 to early 1900s

CAMPHENE LAMP

A lamp, made of metal or glass, designed to burn camphene, a distillation of turpentine, one of the first petroleum products to be developed. Twin wick holders angle away from each other to form a "V". They taper to the tip and grasp the wick very tightly, counteracting the tendency for the flame to follow the wick down into the fuel chamber and cause an explosion. Camphene lamps were equipped with wick covers to prevent evaporation of fuel when the unit was not in use. (See also Peg Lamp and Whale Oil Lamp.)

PLACE: Europe and United States

TIME: 1830 to 1880

CRESSET

An iron pot surrounded by a wrought-iron guard. It can be used as either a candleholder or an oil lamp. When carried on a pole, the cresset is mounted on a swivel and weighted to keep it upright, but more often it is positioned on a stationary wall and used as a wall sconce. (Compare with Moon Lantern.)

SIZE: 7 inches in diameter

PLACE: Europe

TIME: 500 to 1400

CRUSIE

An early open-bodied oil lamp made of cast iron or tin rather than pottery. Its rag wick burns while floating on the surface of the oil. One end of the bowl comes to a point and an attempt is made to lay the wick into this end and to keep it confined there. Some crusies have narrowed points designed into each of the corners and supporting four flaming wicks, significantly increasing the light. The output of smoke and odors is also multiplied by four.

SIZE: 8 to 10 inches long

PLACE: Scotland

TIME: 500s

DECK LANTERN A kerosene lantern for use outdoors. It was employed by both the U.S. Navy and the American railroads for running lights and for signaling.

SIZE: 9 to 12 inches high

PLACE: United States

TIME: 1890s

FUEL OIL A combustible liquid used in lamps. The earliest fuel was lard or grease — animal fats. Exodus 27:20 says: "Command the children of Israel to bring pure oil of pressed olives for the light, to cause the lamp to burn continually." Olive oil was a costly fuel, but animal fat had its problems too. Lard was solid at room temperature, requiring the wick to lie right in the puddle of warmed oil. Animal fats and vegetable oils were the mainstay fuels till the close of the 18th century when the oil from the sperm whale was produced in quantity. Whale oil was thick, but it worked well with the double-wicked enclosed lamps produced at that time. Camphene, made from turpentine, was produced in the 1830s. Petroleum fuels, paraffin, and kerosene were formulated in the 1860s.

MODERATOR LAMP A lamp with a spring-driven mechanism to force oil from the reservoir to the burning wick. This is one of a series of attempts in the mid-1800s to feed oil lamps with greater quantities of fuel than can be achieved by osmosis.

SIZE: 12 inches high

PLACE: United States

TIME: Invented in 1836

MOON LANTERN A round lantern mounted on a short pole. This lantern was carried by a servant to light the pathway from a carriage to the steps of his master's home. (Compare with Cresset Lamp.)

SIZE: Lamp - 9 inches high, pole - 5 feet

PLACE: Europe, particularly England

TIME: 1500s

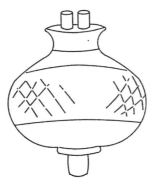

PEG LAMP A lamp fount made of cast glass. In the manufacture of this lamp the glass blower forms a peg-shaped blob of glass on the bottom of the container that will fit into any of the many candlesticks in use at this period. The neck of the container is fitted with a cork holding a pair of metal wick supports. The peg lamp has the great advantage of being spill-proof. It is fueled by either camphene or whale oil.

SIZE: 4½ inches in diameter

PLACE: Europe and United States

TIME: Late 1700s to late 1800s

PHOEBE LAMP An oil lamp consisting of two crusie dishes of slightly different sizes, one mounted just below the other. The lower vessel catches oil that might otherwise splash or seep out from the main fount. The Phoebe lamp minimizes waste and is a step toward a cleaner floor.

SIZE: 8 to 10 inches long

PLACE: Europe and United States

TIME: 1100 to 1400

RUSH LIGHT A wrought-iron holder to grip burning rush reeds or splints of flaming wood. If reeds are used, they are soaked in animal fats, lighted at the top end, and burned like a candle. If wooden splints are used, they are lighted on the lower side and burned to the top. The rush light needs constant attention, repositioning the reed and snuffing out flaming debris as it falls from the holder. Sometimes a tray of water is put under the rush light to catch stray flames that could otherwise be dangerous. Rush lights are so simple and inexpensive that they found considerable use into the 18th century in the American colonies.

PLACE: Worldwide

TIME: Prehistoric to colonial times

SCONCE Originally, a candlestick or torch mounted on a wall. The term now covers any wall-mounted lamp, including those powered by electricity. In the 18th century, pier glasses were flanked with wall sconces, holding candles. In this arrangement the mirror not only reflects my lady's face but also reflects the flame, increasing its brilliance. Today's wall sconces are usually mounted just above eye level. The lamp in the illustration is electric and is from the 1930s.

PLACE: Worldwide

TIME: Medieval times to the present

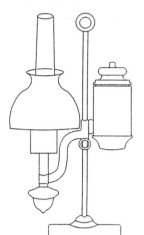

STUDENT LAMP   A desk lamp that provides light suitable for reading and study. The first student lamp was a type of Argand lamp, having a large capacity oil reservoir placed high on a lamp stand. In this position the wick is fed by gravity, and the fount does not cast an objectionable shadow on the work area. The student lamp is adjustable on its stand and can be raised or swiveled to direct light to the best possible working position.

SIZE: 12 to 15 inches high

PLACE: Europe and United States

TIME: 1800s

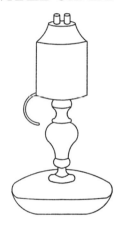

WHALE OIL LAMP   A lamp with a completely enclosed fount, made of metal or glass, and fitted with a double wick designed to burn whale oil. Whale oil burned brighter than animal fats, produced less smoke, and remained liquid at room temperatures. With a slight conversion this lamp could also burn the newer, more volatile camphene.

SIZE: 6 to 9 inches high

PLACE: Europe and United States

TIME: 1780s

WICK   A cord or bundle of cotton threads to carry and control fuel oil as it burns in a lamp. The first wicks were made of moss, plant fiber, or rushes soaked in grease or animal fats. Rags were used at an early date. Cotton was woven in patterns especially for use as lamp wicks in the middle of the 18th century. Betty lamps and whale oil lamps used cotton ropes of various sizes; the Argand lamp required a thickly woven sleeve of cotton; and the kerosene lamp needed a wide, flat woven ribbon.

Brief History of the Lamp	
Reeds soaked in animal grease are burned for light	prehistory
Oil lamp made of pottery is developed	2000 B.C.
Crusie, Phoebe, and Betty lamps are developed	Middle Ages
Whale oil is produced in quantity	1780
Argand invents a lamp with a circular wick	1784
Argand's laboratories design a lamp with a glass chimney	1785
Coal gas is used as a fuel in early gas lights	1792
Gas street lighting appears in both Europe and the United States	1850
Electric arc light is invented	1808
Camphene is marketed	1830
Friction matches are invented	1830
Kerosene and petroleum oils are invented	1854
Edison invents the incandescent light bulb	1879
Electric light bulb is marketed	1880
Electric light socket with pull chain	1896
Flashlight is invented	turn of the century
Fluorescent tube is developed and marketed	1934

Matches

STARTING FIRES

Fires were very difficult to start before the invention of matches. Rubbing two sticks together will surely start a fire, but it can only be done by someone who is highly skilled in the process. Early on, a man might find himself begging at his neighbor's door for a few hot coals if his fire went out. Sending a shower of sparks in a bed of dry moss by striking two flint stones is a method needing less skill but still requiring a measure of patience. Relics have been found indicating that a glass lens was known in Egypt, but it was not in wide use as a burning glass until glass-blowing was perfected. The 18th century pipe smoker had to transfer flames from the fireplace to his bowl with a lighted sliver of wood. The first phosphorus matches produced were poisonous, causing a condition known as necrosis. Thousands of people died from breathing phosphorus fumes in the seventy years it took to perfect a safe compound.

BOOK MATCHES A paperboard comb of safety matches made in rows of ten and bound in a folding paper cover. The exterior of the cover carries the striking surface. When closed, the cover protects the unused matches from accidental ignition.

PLACE: United States

TIME: Patented in 1892

Widely distributed by 1915

BURNING GLASS A lens made of glass and used to focus the sun's rays to a small spot on a piece of tinder, thereby starting a fire. Archeologists have found, dated to Early Egypt, lenses capable of starting fires.

PLACE AND TIME: Egypt - 1200 B.C.

Egypt - 150 A.D.

England, Westminster Abbey - 1388 A.D.

BUTANE LIGHTER A cigarette lighter fueled by butane gas. The first butane lighter could be refilled. An inexpensive butane lighter that can be disposed of when empty became very popular, nearly replacing lighters that burn lighter fluid.

PLACE: United States

TIME: Refillable - 1945

Disposable - 1975

CONGREVE   A friction match, tipped with antimony sulfide, chlorate of potash, and gum arabic. (See also Lucifer.)

PLACE: England

TIME: Introduced in 1827

FLINT AND TINDER   A fire-starting kit consisting of a canister, flint, steel striker, tinder, and kindling. A shower of sparks is produced by striking the flint with a steel scraper (or a very hard rock). Sparks fall on the parched cotton tinder (dry moss or dried bark from certain trees), causing it to smoke. The smoulder is fanned and fed with splinters, producing a flame. This primitive technology was in use till matches were perfected. The kit in this drawing is from the early 1800s.

PLACE: Worldwide

TIME: Prehistory to the present

LUCIFER   An early match requiring a lot of friction to ignite. The supply of matches comes with a sheet of sandpaper for striking. The sandpaper is wrapped around the match head and held with one hand while the other hand jerks the stem of the match out of the tight sandpaper blanket. The lucifer goes off with a sort of explosion accompanied by a shower of sparks.

PLACE: United States

TIME: Introduced in 1835

MATCHSAFE   A box for holding and carrying a personal supply of strike-anywhere matches. The matchsafe protects the tip of the match from contacting coins, keys, or other metal in the user's pocket. It comes with a flip-open end-piece and looks a lot like a small cigarette case. These boxes were produced in quantities, printed with advertisements, and distributed as giveaways.

SIZE: 3 inches long, 1½ inches wide, ³/₈ inch thick

PLACE: United States

TIME: Introduced in 1895

SAFETY MATCH   A match designed with the igniting chemical painted on the exterior of the box. It cannot be lighted accidentally by touching and rubbing other objects.

PLACE AND TIME: Invented in Sweden, 1844

Distributed worldwide in the 1850s

Brief History of Fire Ignition

Flint and tinder	earliest times
Burning glass is in general use	150 A.D.
Chemical fire-starting kits are produced; they are crude and dangerous	1680
First friction match is invented and produced	1827
Phosphorus strike-anywhere matches invented; they are widely distributed and poisonous	1830
Safety matches requiring a chemical striking surface are introduced	1852
Advertisements first appear on a matchbook cover	1898
Non-toxic strike-anywhere matches are produced	1911
Cigarette lighters are introduced	1909
Book matches become popular during World War I	1914
Refillable butane lighters are marketed	1945
Disposable butane lighters become widely popular	1975

Writing Tools and Supplies

PENS, PENCILS, AND OTHERS

BALLPOINT PEN A pen having a small ball bearing that rolls through an ink reservoir and deposits the ink as it rolls over a writing surface. The concept of the ballpoint was invented in 1888.

PLACE: Worldwide

TIME: Practical version marketed in 1940

BULL A letter, an edict, or an official document from the Pope.

BULLA An official seal attached to a document. The Papal bull uses a round leaden seal.

ENVELOPE A paper sleeve that can be glued shut and used as a container for letters. Before the envelope was developed, the letter was folded in thirds and sealed with sealing wax.

PLACE AND TIME: Invented in New York City - 1839

Window envelopes invented in 1902

ERASER A device for removing pencil, ink, or chalk marks from paper. Rubber got its name when it was *rubbed* across pencil marks and found to be effective in removing them.

PLACE AND TIME: Discovered in England - 1770

First mounted on the end of a pencil in 1858

FELT MARKER A pen with a self-contained ink reservoir and a felt tip. When the felt marker was introduced, it was immediately accepted.

PLACE: Worldwide

TIME: Invented and first marketed in 1960

FOUNTAIN PEN A pen in which an ink supply in a reservoir is fed to the writing nib. The fountain pen was first manufactured for consumer use by Lewis Edson Waterman.

PLACE: United States

TIME: 1884

MECHANICAL PENCIL A pencil that has the graphite core placed in a metal housing. The mechanical pencil usually allows the lead to be retracted into the housing.

PLACE: Europe and United States

TIME: Introduced in the 1800s

PAPER A thin flexible writing material made from the pulp of rags, straw, or wood.

PLACE AND TIME: Invented in China - 105 A.D.

Linen developed in Iraq - 800 A.D.

Paper introduced to Europe - 1100

PAPYRUS A writing material made of strips of pith from the papyrus plant. The strips are laid very close together in orderly rows across similar strips in a thin layer. The mat is soaked and dried under great pressure. Papyrus was also used by the Egyptians as a fabric for making mats, sandals, and sailcloth.

PLACE: Egypt

TIME: 2500 B.C.

PARCHMENT An animal skin prepared as a surface for writing. Parchment is usually made from sheep or goat skin. The hair is removed, the hide is tanned, and then both sides are polished to be flexible and capable of receiving inks.

PLACE AND TIME: Animal skins - 2000 B.C.

Double-sided parchment produced - 160 B.C.

PEN A device used in writing or drawing with ink. At first, slit and pointed bamboo reeds were used to apply the ink. Bird quills superseded the reed, and finally, steel nib pens replaced the quill.

PLACE AND TIME: Reed pens - Egypt - 2000 B.C.

Quill pens - Europe - 1250 A.D.

Steel nibs - England - 1809 A.D.

PENCIL A rod-shaped instrument, usually made of wood, with a core of graphite and clay or crayon. Romans used pencils that actually had a core of lead.

PLACE: Europe, particularly France, Germany, and England

TIME: Invented in 1500

PORTABLE WRITING DESK A slant-top lapbox that sits on the knees of a seated person and is used as a writing surface. The top is a lid that hinges open to provide a storage space for necessary writing materials. The box has two wells to hold an ink bottle and drying powder. In the studio, the writing desk sits on a table and is at a convenient height for holding writing papers.

SIZE: 14 by 20 by 5 inches

PLACE: Europe, particularly Germany

TIME: 1400s to 1700s

QUILL A large, stiff bird feather trimmed to a point and split to accept a load of ink. Turkey, goose, and duck quill pens replaced wood and reed styluses for writing on paper and on parchment skins.

The quill is sharpened with four strokes of a knife blade. The first cuts diagonally across the stem of the feather, the second and third refine the point, and the last cut makes a slit up the stem to transport the ink to the tip.

1st Cut   2nd and 3rd Cut   4th Cut and finished pen

The quill was still in use as recently as the early 1900s for signing ceremonial documents.

PLACE: Worldwide

TIME: Introduced in 1250

SCROLL A message or a lengthy manuscript written on a roll of parchment, paper, or other material. The scroll may be rolled either vertically or horizontally.

SIZE: 1 inch diameter, 10 inches long to 4 inches diameter, 24 inches long

PLACE AND TIME: Papyrus - Egypt - 1000 B.C.

Parchment - Rome - 500 B.C.

Silk paper - China - 100 A.D.

TYPEWRITER A writing machine. When keys are struck, letters are pressed against an inked ribbon leaving an impression on paper. Remington bought the rights to this invention, improved the machine, and manufactured it.

PLACE: Worldwide, particularly United States

TIME: Invented in 1867

Marketed in 1873

Electric typewriter was marketed in 1956

VELLUM A fine grade parchment (see Parchment) made from the skins of newborn or stillborn calves.

WRITING BRUSH A thin-tipped brush, dipped in ink and used as a writing instrument.

PLACE: China

TIME: 2500 B.C.

Brief History of Writing Tools and Supplies

Egyptians make and use papyrus	2500 B.C.
Egyptians and Chinese invent ink, applied with a brush	2500 B.C.
Wooden stylus and split reeds are used as pens	2000 B.C.
Animal skins are prepared for use as a writing surface	2000 B.C.
Double-sided parchment is introduced in Europe	160 B.C.
Chinese produce paper made of bark and hemp fiber	150 B.C.
Chinese first produce paper for writing purposes	110 A.D.
Chinese develop a process for woodblock printing	600
Spain and Italy set up and operate paper mills	1250
Quill-and-ink is first used for writing	1250
Johann Gutenberg invents the printing press	1454
Fountain pen is invented	1780
Envelope is invented in New York City	1839
Steel nib pens are available to replace the quill	1850
Rubber eraser is attached to a pencil	1858
Typewriter is marketed by Remington	1873
Practical fountain pen is widely marketed	1884
Ballpoint pen is invented	1888
Ballpoint pen is improved and marketed	1940
Electric typewriter is marketed	1956
Felt-tip marking pen is widely marketed	1960

Eyeglasses

EARLY EYEGLASSES

Roger Bacon is credited with inventing the first eyeglass for the western world, in the latter part of the 13th century. This device was a single magnifying lens held in front of the eye by means of a short handle. By the 14th century, kings, clergymen, and members of the upper classes were using spectacles that had two lenses. These early glasses were large and awkward, giving the appearance that the user was holding an inverted pair of scissors to his eyes.

In the early part of the 16th century, the printing press made reading material plentiful. The elderly complained that their close-range vision was not what they wanted it to be. A widespread need for corrective glasses produced a new craft — spectacle making.

The monocle and the lorgnette, hand-held eyeglasses, became fashionable among the ladies and gentlemen of the courts of Europe in the middle of the 17th century, even when there was no corrective need. The spectacles of this period were either clipped to the bridge of the nose or tied to the wearer's head with leather straps.

Lightweight thin metal frames were worn by Benjamin Franklin, and the style continued unchanged for 150 years, remaining standard into the 1930s.

BIFOCALS A pair of spectacles having an upper and a lower part in each lens. The upper part of the lens is designed for distance vision and the lower part is ground for close work.

PLACE: Philadelphia, Pennsylvania

TIME: Introduced in 1785, to the present

GRANNY GLASSES Thin metal-rimmed glasses. (See Wire-rimmed Glasses.)

HALF GLASS A pair of glasses for reading and other close work. The lenses are small and designed so the wearer can easily look over the top of the frame to see things in the distance. The glasses in the illustration have adjustable temples.

TIME: Early 1800s to the present

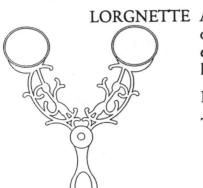

LORGNETTE A pair of spectacles equipped with a handle, to be held in front of the eyes for short periods of time to examine items of interest. The lorgnette was frequently hung from a chain around a lady's neck and was used more for show than vision correction.

PLACE: Europe, particularly France and England

TIME: Early 1700s

MONOCLE An optical lens for one eye. The monocle is held in place by sliding it between the flesh of the upper part of the cheek and the eyebrow.

PLACE AND TIME: Developed and in scattered use - 1600s

In general use in Europe - early 1800s

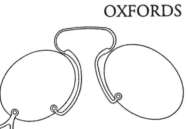

OXFORDS A pair of eyeglasses that clamp to the bridge of the nose as a result of tension supplied by the spring bar that connects the two lenses. (Compare with Pince-Nez.)

PLACE: England and United States

TIME: Early 1900s

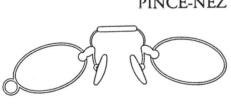

PINCE-NEZ A pair of eyeglasses (frequently frameless) held in place by a pair of spring-actuated pads fastened to the inside edge of each lens. The padded clasp grips the flesh on the bridge of the wearer's nose.

PLACE: Europe, particularly France

TIME: Mid-1800s

QUIZZING GLASS A single-lens magnifying glass. The quizzer was one of the earliest eyeglasses and the forerunner of the lorgnette. It was said that Nero watched the gladiator contests peering through a quizzer containing an emerald as a lens.

TIME: In use as a novelty from 600 B.C. to 1200 A.D.

A practical model was developed in 1280 A.D.

SPECTACLES Any pair of lenses mounted in a lightweight frame and worn in front of the eyes to improve vision.

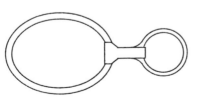

TEMPLES The sidepieces of a pair of glasses. Temples may be designed with straight bars to press against the temples or with bent ends to fit behind the ears.

PLACE AND TIME: Invented in England - 1728

In general use mid-1700s to the present

WIRE-RIMMED GLASSES

Thin metal-rimmed glasses, such as those worn by Santa Claus and your grandmother. There was a renewed interest in this style of glasses in the 1960s, largely due to the fact that Beatles star John Lennon chose to wear this style of frame.

PLACE: Introduced in United States

TIME: Introduced in 1750

Brief History of Eyeglasses

Glass globe is produced capable of starting a fire and of magnification	1200 B.C.
Chinese make folding wooden frames for eyeglasses	600 A.D.
Egyptians grind a lens specifically for magnification	1038
Roger Bacon suggests a concave lens for vision improvement	1268
First practical spectacles are produced	1280
Charles V of France wears black horn-rimmed glasses	1379
English Spectacle-Makers Guild receives its first charter	1563
Edward Scarlett, English spectacle maker, invents temples	1728
Benjamin Franklin invents the bifocal lens	1785
Monocle is in general use	1800
French develop the pince-nez	mid-1800s
Contact lens is marketed	1948

Hearing Aids

EARLY INSTRUMENTS

Although instruments to improve sight came to be thought of as quaint and fashionable, the instruments to improve hearing were not. Hearing disorders were considered an affliction, and ear trumpets were conspicuous and awkward. Most people attempted to conceal their hearing aids and to minimize any focus on their ailment. Others, especially the aged, readily admitted their problem and used anything that would assist.

HEARING FAN A woman might use her fan in a coy way, gathering sound waves and directing them to her ear, in much the same way that you might cup your hand guiding and amplifying the sound. With certain ear ailments, a paper or celluloid fan could be held against the teeth, causing the teeth and connecting bone structure to vibrate enough to hear speech and music without distortion of the sound.

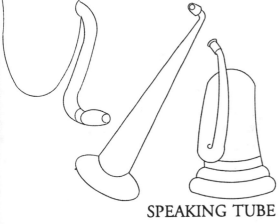

HEARING TRUMPET A tin trumpet used by the hard of hearing to increase the number of sound waves reaching the ear. The hearing trumpet was made by a tinsmith and was sold in stores and by peddlers of pots and pans. Some trumpets were large and obvious. Other versions were designed in a more compact arrangement. They could be almost concealed as they were held in the hand.

SIZE: 12 to 14 inches long (large model)

5 inches (compact model)

PLACE: Europe and United States

TIME: 1800s to 1930s

SPEAKING TUBE A hose for direct communication with one person. The speaking tube was the most apparent aid to hearing and was usually used only when a hearing trumpet was not successful.

Electronic hearing aids based on the principle of the telephone were introduced in the 1930s. The first wearable electronic hearing aid was marketed in 1935. It was large, and attempts were made to hide it in the user's clothing. These instruments consisted of three basic parts—the transmitter, the receiver, and a battery pack. Rheostats were supplied to allow the user some control over the incoming sounds. He could vary the volume according to individual requirements.

Appliances

——— BROOMS AND VACUUM CLEANERS ———

The modern broom is not so different from the brooms made in the distant past. Broomcorn native to Africa was imported to the United States in the middle of the 18th century and was grown especially for use in brooms, but the technology was no different from when small twigs or reeds were tightly bound to a 4-foot broomstick.

CARPET SWEEPER A mechanical carpet sweeper was the first major improvement in floor cleaning since the broom. It has a rotating brush that catchs surface dirt, sweeping it into a self-contained dustpan.

TIME: 1876

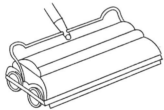

The early carpet cleaners working on a sucking principle were manually operated. One model had a hand-turned turbine; one hand turned the crank, the other hand operated the vacuum hose. Another model had a bellows mounted near the floor that was operated with a long handle. A third model worked on the principle of a hand-operated piston. None of these attempts was practical so very few were sold.

Motors in 1900 had to be large in order to be powerful, and turbine technology was slow in coming. The first successful vacuum cleaner was so large it had to be mounted on a four-wheeled wagon and could not fit through a standard door. This commercial machine required a crew of two people to operate and was used for cleaning restaurants, theaters, churches, etc. It could only be used in a home with the aid of a long hose. A true home version of this large model was introduced in 1910, but it had to be stationary and reside in the basement with hose connections mounted along the baseboards throughout the house.

SUCTION SWEEPER An upright vacuum cleaner called a "Suction Sweeper" was marketed by the Hoover Company. This style of cleaner continues to be popular to the present day.

TIME: 1909

Brief History of Brooms and Vacuum Cleaners	
Broomcorn is grown in America for broom production	mid-1700s
Manually operated suction cleaners are introduced	1870s
Melvin Bissel is granted a patent for a mechanical carpet sweeper	1876
Motor-driven vacuum cleaner is patented	1897
Commercial vacuum cleaner is developed in England	1901
Fuller Brush Company begins selling door to door	1905
Upright electric vacuum cleaner is introduced by Hoover	1909
Central vacuum cleaners are installed in basements	1910
Tank type vacuum cleaner is marketed by Electrolux	1924

CAN OPENERS

The idea of storing meat in sealed glass jars came from the fact that wine was so well preserved in bottles. Napoleon fed his troops in the field with canned food. A process for packing food in tin cans was perfected in England in 1828. The can opener was invented some thirty years later. The early manufacturer recommended that his cans be opened with a "chisel and hammer" or a strongly built knife. The northern soldiers in the Civil War used a bayonet. Fish canneries sprang up in California and Maine. A fish can was invented with a built-in opening strip operated with an enclosed key. As canning improved and a thinner sheet tin was used in constructing the container, the common pocket knife was the accepted can opener. The habit of using a pocket knife continued to the middle of the 20th century.

ROUND BLADE A rotary blade forced through the tin can lid by a spurred wheel was invented as an improvement over the straight steel blade. The principle of the rotary blade continues to be used on all can openers, including the electric models.

TIME: 1870

STEEL BLADE The first tool designed specifically to open cans was a steel blade mounted in a wood handle. Once it was invented it served well. This style of opener is still available in stores today.

TIME: 1858

Brief History of the Can Opener

Sealing food in cans to prevent spoilage is invented in France	1810
Canning industry is introduced to the United States	1817
Fish cannery opens in California	1850s
Blade can opener is invented	1858
Fish can with a built-in keyed opening strip is introduced	1866
Can opener with a rotary knife blade is introduced	1870
Wall-mounted can opener is marketed	1927
Electric can opener is available	1956

CLOTHES IRONS

A clothes iron is a device made of iron with a smooth under-surface, heated and used for pressing cloth to remove wrinkles and make pleats. The Greeks and Romans pleated their gowns by rolling a heated wheel over the dampened fold. Europeans used a charcoal-heated flatiron during the Renaissance in their quest for wrinkle-free clothing. A flatiron heated on a stove or at a fireplace did a satisfactory job of smoothing cotton clothing if it did not dirty the fabric with soot it collected from the fire.

ELECTRIC IRON The iron was one of the first appliances to go electric. Working models of the electric iron were developed even before electricity was generally available.

TIME: 1882

GAS IRON When gas lighting came to the cities, the flatiron was quick to be heated with the new energy source. The gas heated iron was a short-lived item: before the problems of temperature control and safety could be worked out, electricity arrived on the scene.

TIME: 1894

SAD IRON Ironing is particularly tiring when it is done with a sad iron. Sad, in this case, means compact or heavy, and these early irons could weigh as much as ten pounds. With all its inconvenience, however, the flatiron or sad iron was used into the 20th century in the United States until electrical wiring reached the rural parts of the country.

TIME: 1700s to 1930s

Brief History of Clothes Irons	
Early roller for pressing pleats is used in Ancient Greece	300 B.C.
Charcoal-heated iron is developed in Europe	1500s
Stove-heated flatiron is standard	1700s to 1930s
Patent is granted for an electric iron	1882
Gas-heated flatiron is invented	1894
"Hotpoint" iron is on the market	1906
Adjustable automatic thermostat is developed	1927
Steam iron is developed and marketed	1930

COFFEEMAKERS

The coffee bean was introduced to Europe in the 16th century, and for three hundred years the drink was made by boiling some grounds in water until it "smelled good."

BIGGIN  The first coffeemaker was a dripolator, developed in France under the name of Biggin. The top of this two-part unit contained coffee grounds and was separated from the bottom by a filter. Boiling water was poured over the grounds and slowly dripped through the coffee and the filter. For the first time the grounds were kept separate from the beverage.

PLACE: France

TIME: 1800s

COFFEE BOILER  The coffee boiler in the illustration is from the turn of the 20th century and is made of blue enameled steel. Such a pot can still be purchased today. Coffee grounds unavoidably mix in with the drink and collect in the bottom of the cup.

PLACE: Europe and United States

TIME: 1500s to 1900s

PERCOLATOR  A two-part coffeemaker divided by a filter. The grounds are contained in the upper part. The difference between this maker and the dripolator is what the company calls a cold water pump. Coffee-making begins with cold water in the bottom of the pot. As the water boils, it is forced up a tube to flow over the grounds and back to the bottom of the pot. This process of "perking" the water up the tube and through the coffee continues until the coffee is done.

TIME: 1908

SILEX COFFEEMAKER

Silex developed the "vacuum drip," an innovation in coffee-making. An airtight seal was made between the bottom and top units. Water boiled in the lower chamber generates steam, forcing the water up a tube into the upper chamber. After it dripped one time through the grounds, it was "coffee time."

Brief History of Coffee Makers	
Biggin dripolator is introduced in France	1800
Percolator is developed and marketed	1908
Silex makes an all-glass coffeemaker	1914
Silex develops the vacuum drip coffeemaker	1940

MIXERS AND BLENDERS

Mixers and blenders are characterized by a motor-driven beater that can mix drinks, stir cakes, grind coffee, and/or liquefy fruits and vegetables.

BLENDER

A cocktail mixer, developed by band leader Fred Waring, was marketed to bartenders. Later this blender is refined and put on the market as a fruit and vegetable liquefier. Even with the help of nutritionists and food authorities, it took ten years and a world war for the food blender to catch on.

TIME: 1936

BLENDER WITH SPEED
CONTROLS

When speed controls were added to the blender, a lively competition developed as to which manufacturer could install the most buttons. After nine years, and a close race, the winner was Waring, who managed to install fifteen speeds, including "off."

TIME: 1960s

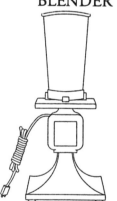

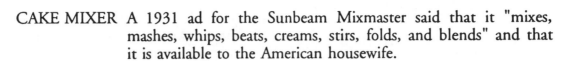

CAKE MIXER A 1931 ad for the Sunbeam Mixmaster said that it "mixes, mashes, whips, beats, creams, stirs, folds, and blends" and that it is available to the American housewife.

TIME: 1931

MALT MIXER Hamilton Beach was the first on the market with a high speed fractional horsepower motor that drove a small disk with four to six vanes for the single intended purpose of making malted milk drinks. These were commercially marketed to drug store soda fountains.

PLACE: Racine, Wisconsin

TIME: 1924

Brief History of Mixers and Blenders	
Hamilton Beach markets a mixer for making malted milkshakes	1924
Sunbeam markets its first Mixmaster	1931
Waring Blender is marketed as a cocktail mixer	1936
Food processor is offered to the public by Waring	1940
Food processor is generally accepted	1950s
Dormeyey, Oster, Waring, and others compete in the pushbutton war	1963 to 1972

PHONOGRAPHS AND RECORDINGS

The home entertainment industry began with Thomas Edison's invention of the cylinder recorder and has grown in leaps. Every generation a major development in technology has produced a format change. As new equipment is purchased for the home, the old equipment is rendered obsolete.

In 1900, as soon as they were available to the public, the wind-up gramophone and Victrola were popular. Twenty-five years later, the phonograph, taking advantage of new technology, went all electric. Another twenty-five years brought high fidelity and the 33 rpm format. Twenty years more saw a major revolution. The cassette tape player became king, and we paid homage by sending our old records to Goodwill. Right now, the compact disc (CD) player rules, but there are rumblings on the frontier being made by something called the DAT (Digital Audio Tape). No one can know when the current reign will end, but if history is any teacher we can expect a new development — and soon.

Brief History of Phonographs and Recordings	
Edison invents the cylinder recorder	1878
Gramophone, a disc record player, is invented in Germany	1886
Gramophone is marketed in America	1887
Victrola, a U.S. version of the Gramophone, is marketed	1900s
All electric 78 rpm phonograph is developed	1925
Coin-operated jukebox is introduced	1925
All electric jukebox is marketed	1927
Magnetic tape recording is invented in Germany	1935
High fidelity record is produced in England	1944
Reel-to-reel magnetic tape recorder is marketed	1947
Wire recording is developed for the home market	1948
First long-playing record (33 rpm) is marketed	1948
RCA introduces the first 45 rpm record	1949
Radio-phonograph console (78, 45, and 33 rpm) is marketed	1950
Stereophonic recording is developed	1958
Cassette tape player is on the market	1963
Microcassette pocket recorder is marketed by Olympus	1976
Walkman portable cassette player by Sony is available	1979
Compact disc (CD) is introduced	1980

REFRIGERATORS

A refrigerator is defined here as any space, room, or box that is cooled for the purpose of storing food and keeping it from spoiling. The earliest such space was cooled with blocks of ice. The Chinese cut and stored ice for refrigeration 3000 years ago. American colonists had the foresight to cut ice in the winter and store it in ice sheds for summer use.

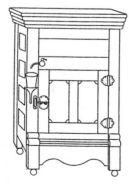

ICE BOX A new piece of kitchen furniture, the ice box, was introduced shortly after ice-making plants began producing 50-pound blocks of ice.

TIME: 1870s

MECHANICAL REFRIGERATOR

The first practical mechanical refrigerator was invented in the late 19th century. A small model for domestic use was marketed by the Domelre Company. The refrigeration unit on this early model was mounted on top of the box in full view.

TIME: 1913

Once the mechanism was hidden, with the motor and compressor housed in the lower part of the cabinet and the coils located to the rear, the refrigerator was much more attractive.

Brief History of Refrigerators	
Chinese cut and store ice for refrigeration purposes	1000 B.C.
American colonists store ice in ice sheds	1600s
Ice is shipped from New York to southern ports and California	1800s
First commercial plant for making ice blocks	1868
Ice boxes are marketed for home pantries	1870s
Ice is home delivered	1870 to 1930s
Electric refrigerator for home use is marketed	1913
Kelvinator and Frigidaire produce home refrigerators	1919
Decorator colors are available	1960s

SAFETY RAZORS

A safety razor is any razor with a guard to reduce the possibility of nicking the skin.

STRAIGHT-EDGED SAFETY RAZOR

The first safety razor is straight-edged and has a guard on one side.

TIME: 1762

"T" RAZOR

The first razor with the familiar "T" shape was introduced more than 100 years later. It had a permanent blade that needed periodic resharpening.

TIME: 1880

Disposable blades were conceived and developed by King Gillette at the turn of the 20th century. Working against the advice of close friends and associates, he manufactured and distributed his version of the safety razor.

An electrically powered razor with blades that cut like miniature shears was introduced a quarter of a century later. The electric razor allowed a man to shave with a dry face—a welcome event when he had only cold water or no water at all.

Brief History of Safety Razors

First razor with a guard is invented in France	1762
"T"-shaped razor is introduced in the United States	1880
Gillette invents and markets disposable razor blades	1901
Schick patents an electric razor	1928
Schick's razor is marketed	1931
Remington designs an electric shaver especially for women	1940
Remington introduces a razor powered by an automobile's cigarette lighter	1940
Cordless razor with rechargeable batteries is marketed	1960

SEWING MACHINES

The first sewing machine was built in England for stitching leather. It had a hook instead of an eye, used a single thread, and made a chain stitch similar to that in crocheting. It was not practical for sewing cloth. A machine invented to sew French uniforms during the reign of King Louis XVI made a straight seam six times faster than a tailor could by hand. The tailors of the time considered this machine to be a threat to their livelihood.

The sewing machine as we know it today was invented by Elias Howe. It made a lock stitch and used two threads, one housed in a bobbin. Howe's machine ran as you turned a crank with one hand. Isaac Singer made improvements in Howe's design and added a foot-operated treadle so both hands were free to handle the cloth. In the early days of electricity, the first motors developed were comparatively slow and lacking in power—perfect for adaptation to the sewing machine.

Brief History of Sewing Machines

Machine for stitching leather is developed in England	1790
Sewing machine is invented in France to sew army uniforms	1830
Elias Howe invents the prototype of today's sewing machine	1846
Isaac Singer makes improvements and adds a treadle	1851
Singer sewing machine is motorized	1889

TOASTERS

A toaster is a device for roasting bread to make it crisp. The Egyptian toasted bread to reduce its moisture and preserve it from spoiling. The Roman put pieces of charred bread in his wine cup to reduce acidity. The English make fried bread in a skillet. Today, toast is eaten as a breakfast food in England and the United States.

ELECTRIC TOASTER An open rack toaster powered by an electric heating unit was marketed by both Westinghouse and General Electric. Sitting on the breakfast table, it saved many steps in the kitchen.

TIME: 1910

POP-UP TOASTER An automatic toaster was developed by Toastmaster. The toaster in the illustration has two controls: one turns on the current, the other sets a timer. It toasts one slice of bread.

TOASTING RACK An early toaster, holding four slices of bread, was heated over a wood or coal stove. The rod and wire framework gently clamped the slices, tilting them into the center of the heat. It toasted only one side.

TIME: Mid-1800s

Brief History of Toasters	
Rack is designed to toast bread on a wood stove	mid-1800s
Electric toaster is developed to sit on a breakfast table	1910
Automatic pop-up toaster is marketed	1926
"Toast-R-oven" by General Electric is marketed	1956

TOOTHBRUSHES

The first toothbrush was made of hog bristles. Synthetic bristles made of nylon were introduced in 1938.

ELECTRIC TOOTHBRUSH

The first electrically powered toothbrush was produced after World War II. It enjoyed a minor success primarily overseas.

PLACE: Switzerland

TIME: 1950s

The rights for United States distribution of this toothbrush were acquired in 1960 by Squibb and Sons; it was marketed under the name Broxodent.

General Electric developed the first cordless toothbrush, powered by rechargeable batteries.

WATER PIC

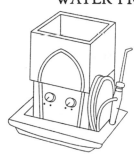

A pulsing water jet for cleaning the teeth was developed and marketed by Water Pic.

PLACE: United States

TIME: 1966

Brief History of Toothbrushes	
Dr. West's Miracle Tuft Toothbrush, the first with synthetic bristles, is introduced	1938
First electric toothbrush is produced in Switzerland	1950s
Broxodent electric brush is marketed in the U.S.	1960
Cordless toothbrush is developed by General Electric	1961
Water Pic is on the market	1966

WASHING MACHINES

For centuries, clothing was washed by beating it with a paddle and rubbing it on large flat rocks in a running stream. American colonists brought the job closer to home, heating their wash in a kettle and wringing it out by hand.

CRANK-OPERATED WASHER

A crank-operated washer allowed the housewife to do the washing without getting her hands in hot water.

TIME: Late 1800s

WASH TUB/SCRUB BOARD

The wash tub/scrub board combination was in use in the middle of the 19th century. Washing clothes could be done with a minimum of mess on the back porch.

TIME: 1830s to 1930s

WASHER-WRINGER

An electric washing machine with a round tub and a top-mounted wringer was developed and was truly labor-saving. This style washer with minor design refinements is still available today, for use in car washes and industrial applications.

TIME: 1907 to the present

Brief History of Washing Machines	
Scrub board is patented	1830
Wash tub/scrub board/wringer combination is in use	1840s
Crank-operated rotary motion washer is invented in France	1845
Crank-operated washing machine is introduced to America	late 1800s
Thor markets the first electric washer	1907
Spin dryer is introduced to America	1924
First Wash-a-teria is open for business in Fort Worth, Texas	1934

—————————— MISCELLANEOUS APPLIANCES ——————————

Brief History of Miscellaneous Appliances	
Ice cream freezer is invented	1864
Ice cream freezer hits a peak in popularity	1915
Dishwasher is patented by Josephine Cochrane	1886
Cochrane's machine is on the market for restaurant use	1895
Cochrane's machine comes out in a home model	1914
KitchenAid markets an improved dishwasher	1950
Electric fan is developed and marketed	1904
Electric heating pad is invented	1912
Microwave cooker is invented	1947
Microwave oven is improved and marketed	1967
Electric blanket is patented (has problems with fire and safety)	1937
Electric blanket is improved and marketed by Simmons	1946
Electronic calculators made in Japan flood the market	1970

PART II: CIVIL AUTHORITY

Scepters and Crowns
Standards and Flags
Punishments

Scepters and Crowns

ROYAL SYMBOLS

The royal crown and scepter are the symbols of a sovereign's right to lead and have been used by emperors, potentates, medieval magistrates, and kings the world over. Both the scepter and the crown date to antiquity and are still in use by royalty today.

SCEPTERS

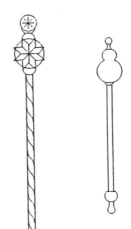

The scepter may be very plain or highly ornamented with precious metals, carvings, and jewels. Both styles have been in service in all periods.

SIZE: 2 to 4 feet high

PLACE: Europe and the Orient

TIME: 3000 B.C. to the present

BAUBLE A short stick surmounted by a fool's head. A court jester's scepter—his symbol of mock authority.

SIZE: 2 feet high

PLACE: Europe

TIME: 1100s to 1400s

CROOK AND FLAIL A pair of articles carried as scepters by Osiris, a good and kindly Egyptian god. The shepherd's crook indicates gentle leadership, the harvesting flail suggests a providing concern. The crook and flail were adopted by Tutankhamen as his royal scepters and they are closely identified with him.

SIZE: 1½ feet high

PLACE: Egypt

TIME: 1400 B.C.

FASCES An axe tied up with a bundle of rods so the hatchet head protrudes from the sheaf. The fasces was carried by the chief magistrates in ancient Rome as a symbol of authority.

SIZE: 3 feet high

PLACE: Rome

TIME: 100 B.C.

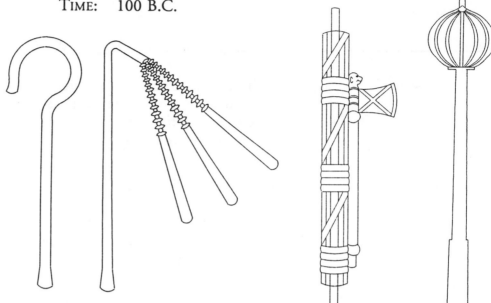

From left to right, Bauble, Crook and Flail, Fasces, Mace

HEQAT A crook, an Egyptian symbol used by both kings and gods. (See Crook and Flail.)

MACE A medieval weapon carried by magistrates and city officials as a scepter to display their right to administer justice. It was not unusual for the local officials of the Middle Ages to use weapons —a sword or a mace—as their badge of authority. The mace was adopted because it so strongly resembled the scepters in current use but was more menacing.

SIZE: 2½ feet high

PLACE: England

TIME: 700s

NEKHAKHA An Egyptian flail, carried by the gods and some of the pharaohs. (See Crook and Flail.)

ORB A round ball with a cross mounted on its summit, carried by royalty in Christian countries. The orb symbolizes the king's secular power on earth, but under the domination of a higher power, that of Christ. Queen Elizabeth I (1558-1603) and Elizabeth II (1952-) both used an orb like the one illustrated on the right.

SIZE: 6 inches in diameter

PLACE: Europe, particularly England

TIME: 1550s to the present

CROWNS

CHAPLET A garland of flowers or a wreath worn on the head.

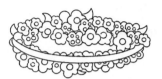

PLACE: Greece and Rome

TIME: 300 B.C. to 200 A.D.

CORONA A crown, especially one given for distinguished military service.

PLACE: Rome

TIME: 100 B.C.

CORONET A small crown denoting noble rank that is less than sovereign. The coronet can also be any chaplet (see Chaplet) or wreath, especially if it is jeweled and intended to be worn on the head.

PLACE: Europe

TIME: 900s to 1500s

CROWN A headgear designed to be worn by royalty. The crown is a symbol of imperial or regal sovereignty.

PLACE: France

TIME: 1000s to 1300s

PLACE: England

TIME: 1500s to the present

DIADEM Any crown or object that resembles a crown.

FRONTLET An ornament worn on the forehead, or a band tied around the head.

GARLAND A wreath or rope of flowers or leaves worn as a token of victory, joy, or honor.

PLACE: Europe

TIME: 300 B.C. to 1600 A.D.

TIARA A richly ornamented coronet of precious metals, jewels, or flowers, worn by women. The tiara is worn even today by the New Year's Day Rose Queen and Miss America. Also a conical cap made of white linen, and worn by the Popes of the 8th, 9th, and 10th centuries.

PLACE: Europe and United States

TIME: 1000s to the present

WREATH A band of flowers or greenery, often worn by a victor.

PLACE: Greece and Rome

TIME: 300 B.C. to 200 A.D.

Standards and Flags

EARLY EXAMPLES

Standards, flags, and coats of arms have been used throughout history to identify a single man with his office, or to identify a body of men with their leader. Mythological gods carried the first standard—a carved symbol mounted atop a rod. Ribbons tied to spears and lances brought identifying color to the early battlefield. The first flag was a piece of colored fabric hanging horizontally from a bar mounted atop a pole. Ships flew flags so others could know their country of origin even if they could not recognize their silhouette. In a similar way medieval knights wore their colors as a cloak on the battlefield to ensure that they were identified by friend and foe alike. A complex system called *heraldry* was devised to control the use of these colors and emblems. Although most of the motivating influences that made heraldry popular are a thing of the past, we have, on a worldwide basis, retained allegiances to national flags.

STANDARDS

The earliest standard was a carved representation of an animal head or a geometric symbol, usually mounted on a staff and carried by the mythological gods of Egypt, Greece, and Rome to show the relationship of the deity with a guardian spirit or totem. The Jews in the Sinai desert were organized into tribes under the leadership of Moses, and each man was identified with the standard of his father's house. The Romans organized their armies into units, each of which proudly carried its own standard.

ANKH A sacred emblem, symbolic of life, carried by many Egyptian gods. The upper portion of the object forms a handle that is easily grasped. The ankh is also known as an Ansate Cross.

SIZE: 6 to 8 inches high

PLACE: Egypt, especially Egyptian mythology

TIME: 3000 B.C.

ANSATE CROSS A cross with a ring handle (see Ankh).

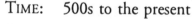

CADUCEUS A winged staff intertwined with two snakes. This staff was carried by Mercury (Hermes), messenger of the gods. The medical profession has claimed the caduceus as its own symbol of healing.

SIZE: 18 inches high

PLACE: Greek and Roman mythology

A striking resemblance is seen as Moses mounts a brazen serpent atop his staff to heal the Israelis of snake bites in their desert wanderings.

PLACE: Sinai Desert

TIME: 1300 B.C.

CROSIER The pastoral staff of the bishop and archbishop of the Catholic Church. The crosier is the bishop's symbol of office but there are times when it precedes him in a procession, being carried by his chaplain.

TIME AND SIZE: 500s to 1200s - 3 to 5 feet high

1200s to the present - 5½ to 6 feet high

PLACE: Rome and Catholic centers

CROSS STAFF A staff associated with the Pope. The staff, carried by an assistant, precedes the Pope in official processions. The Pope is followed by the bishop and his crosier. The staff in the illustration is from the early 1100s.

SIZE: 5 to 6 feet high

PLACE: Europe, particularly Rome, and in Catholic processions

TIME: 500s to the present

From left to right, Crosier (900s, 1000s, 1100s), Cross staff, Ibis staff

IBIS STAFF A rod carried by several of the Egyptian gods — Re, Anubys, Horus, Thor, and others. The top of the staff has a representation of an ibis head, the sacred waterfowl of the Nile.

SIZE: 4½ to 5 feet high

PLACE: Egyptian mythology

LABARUM A standard bearing the monogram of Christ, first carried by Constantine.

SIZE: 7 feet high

PLACE: Rome

TIME: 800s

LITUUS A crooked staff used by ancient priests in divining the future.

SIZE: 2 feet high

PLACE: Rome

TIME: 800 B.C.

PEDUM A stylized shepherd's crook used by an augur, a Roman priest.

SIZE: 4 feet high

PLACE: Rome

TIME: 300 B.C.

THYRSUS A staff tipped with a pine cone. The thyrsus symbolized dominance over the natural realm and was carried by Dionysus, the Satyr, and other Greek gods.

SIZE: 6 feet high

PLACE: Greek mythology

TRIDENT A three-pronged spear carried as a scepter by Poseidon (Neptune), the sea god.

SIZE: 5 feet high

PLACE: Greek and Roman mythology

VEXILLUM A standard assigned to smaller units within the Roman military, especially cavalry units. The eagle, the wreath, and lightning bolts were favorite motifs appearing on Roman standards.

Some Roman vexilloids contained small panels of fabric hanging from a cross bar, an early use of the flag.

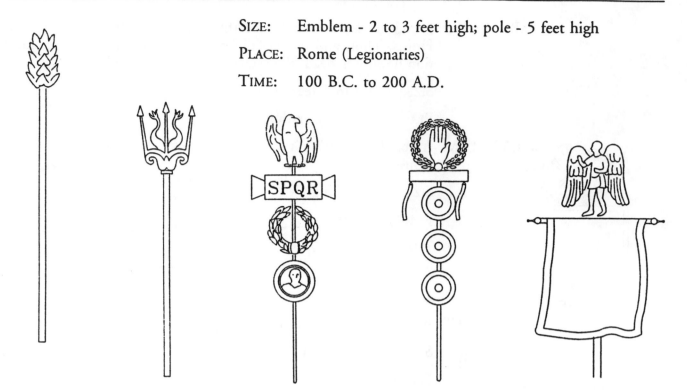

SIZE: Emblem - 2 to 3 feet high; pole - 5 feet high

PLACE: Rome (Legionaries)

TIME: 100 B.C. to 200 A.D.

From left to right, Thyrsus, Trident, Vexillum (3)

FLAGS

Flags made of ribbon, streamers, and fabric were known in early Egyptian times, and cloth funnels and windsocks were flown in early China, but neither of these forms became popular. Roman standards were hung with swatches of fabric, and these evolved in size, shape, and texture, but it wasn't until 1000 A.D. when the Turks carried flags into battle against the Crusaders that men had a true fascination with the colored panels of fabric. The Crusaders brought the idea home and began to use flags in a systematic way. One of the early innovations in flag design was to embroider a prominent emblem in the center of the flag to personalize it. In England of the 15th century, the size and shape of the flag signified the rank of the bearer. The king's flag had square corners, while the flags of his subjects were forked. The royal standard of Henry VII was 30 feet long and tapered toward the fly. The flags of his dukes and knights were smaller according to their rank.

Flags have taken many forms, ranging from long thin streamers to large rectangular blocks of cloth with many different proportions of length and breadth. For instance the Stars and Stripes of America and the Union Jack of England have a ratio of 1:2; the Confederate flag of the South had a ratio of 1:1 and was square; half the state flags of the United States are proportioned 2:3, the other half have proportions unique to each state.

BANDEROLE A long narrow flag or pennant with parallel edges, flown from a masthead or lance. In recent times it refers to a banner carried at a funeral.

BANNER Any flag or standard of a sovereign nation or an army. It is usually displayed hanging from a horizontal pole or suspended between two vertical staffs. (See also Gonfalon.)

BANNERET A small banner carried before a knight showing his embroidered coat of arms. The banner was a display of his rank and title. The knight himself was called a "Knight Banneret."

PLACE: England

TIME: 1400s

BUNTING A string of small flags used for decoration.

BURGEE A triangular or swallow-tail flag used to identify ships.

CANTON A heraldic term for defining the quarters of a flag or shield of arms, especially the upper quarter nearest the flagstaff.

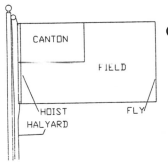

CRAVAT A streamer attached above a flag on the same staff.

ENSIGN A flag flown to identify the national origin of a naval ship. The ship may carry other pennants also.

FIELD The large expanse of a flag on which an emblem is placed.

FLY That portion of a flag farthest from the staff.

HALYARD The rope that is pulled to raise a flag.

HOIST That part of a flag nearest the staff.

GONFALON A battle standard hanging from a horizontal crosspiece. The bottom of the banner is usually cut to form streamers.

PLACE: Italy

TIME: 1300s to 1400s

GUIDON A small pennant carried by the guide of mounted cavalry.

ORIFLAMME The ancient royal standard of France. Made of red silk and trimmed with green fringe, it was split at the bottom edge to form flame-shaped streamers. It was carried into battle by a long succession of kings.

PLACE: France

TIME: 1200s to 1500s

PENCEL   A small flag or streamer.

PENDANT   An alternate spelling for Pennant (see Pennant).

PENNANT   Any long, narrow, triangular flag. Sometimes used as a signal on ships.

PENNON   A pointed or swallow-tailed flag displaying a personal color or emblem worn by a "Knight Bachelor" on his lance. A king may recognize a knight's valor on the field by cutting off the swallow tails, thus promoting him to the rank of "Knight Banneret" (See Banneret.)

PLACE: England

TIME: 1400s

PENNONCEL   A small, narrow pennon or squire's flag on the field of battle.

PLACE: England

TIME: 1400s

SWALLOWTAIL   Any pennon with a "V" shape cut into the leading edge to form two streamers resembling the tail of a swallow.

VANE   A small flag carried by a knight at a tournament. (See also Pennoncel.)

PLACE: Europe, especially France and England

TIME: 1200s

Punishments

DISCIPLINING OFFENDERS

Punishments of the past, in almost every culture and almost every time period, have focused on two goals: to punish the offender and to warn the would-be offender. Executing the punishment in public view carried a threat—if you are caught doing this wrong, you will receive a similar treatment, count on it! The threat was not always accepted in the intended serious light. The crowds drawn to public executions or beatings often were large and experienced the event in a kind of carnival atmosphere.

In the late 1500s, Queen Elizabeth I began banishing convicted criminals, sending them to English plantations in the West Indies and America. In the early 1700s, the practice had parliamentary backing, and prisoners were transported to America on a regular basis. With America's Declaration of Independence in 1776, English prisoners were refused entry at American ports. Still, the English liked the idea, and in 1787 the first load of transported prisoners arrived at Australia.

BASTINADO A small single rod used to punish schoolchildren or military offenders. The bastinado was also appropriate for the Oriental punishment of beating an offender on the soles of his feet.

PLACE: Rome

TIME: 100 A.D.

BIRCH SWITCH A bundle of selected birch twigs, bound together at one end to make a handle. The birch switch was used in schools for disciplining children.

PLACE: England and United States

TIME: 1700s and 1800s

BRANK A metal cage to be locked around the head of a woman convicted of gossiping. The head clamp possessed a metal protrusion that was forced into the victim's mouth. She was chained to a post or tree in a public place.

PLACE: England and colonial America

TIME: 1600s

BULL'S PIZZLE A bull's penis. It was dried, fitted into a handle, and used as a whip.

    PLACE: Europe, particularly England

    TIME: 1400s

CAT-O'-NINE TAILS A whip consisting of nine lashes of rawhide fitted into a single handle. The cords were usually knotted to make each blow more vicious. The cat was used extensively to administer military punishments.

    PLACE: England

    TIME: 1700s to 1800s

COQUEEN STOOL See Cucking Stool.

CUCKING STOOL An open-bottom chair where a woman found guilty of being a common scold was tied. The cucking stool was carried by several men high above their heads and paraded through town for public scorn or ridicule.

    PLACE: England and colonial America

    TIME: 1600s

DUCKING STOOL A chair mounted on a long cantilevered pole for giving a woman convicted of being quarrelsome a controlled dunk into the village well. The punishment was known as *fossa* in Rome, and the bound offenders were dipped into a moat.

    PLACE AND TIME: Rome - 100 A.D.

    England and colonial America - 1600s

FERULE Any flat stick, rod, or cane, used to punish children.

FLAGELLUM A whip made from thongs of ox leather, especially one used to administer religious discipline.

GALLOWS A horizontal beam mounted on a strong frame to execute condemned criminals by hanging. The gallows is erected high atop a scaffold platform to ensure that the event can be viewed by a large audience.

GALLEY A ship propelled by banks of oars. At first the oars were manned by soldiers, then by captured enemy soldiers or slaves, and finally someone thought of sentencing a felon to a term at the galley rather than execution.

PLACE AND TIME: Egypt - 1100 B.C.

Corinth, Greece - 780 B.C.

France - till the mid-1700s

GIBBET A structure with a horizontal beam, resembling a gallows, but intended to display the bodies of criminals who have already been executed. The gibbet was erected and the body was suspended near the site of the crime as a lesson to others.

PLACE: Europe

TIME: 300 B.C. to 1600 A.D.

GIBBET IRONS A suit of iron straps and chains that tightly encircled a corpse to support it while on display. A ring was fastened to the top of the framework and attached to the cross-bar of the gibbet. (See Gibbet for illustration.)

GUILLOTINE A machine for beheading condemned persons with a weighted blade sliding between upright guides.

PLACE: France

TIME: Introduced in 1792

HALIFAX GIBBET A heavy blade mounted in a vertical track for beheading condemned criminals. This device was an early version of what was to become the French guillotine (see Guillotine). Do not confuse the Halifax gibbet with a Gibbet (see Gibbet).

PLACE: Halifax, England

TIME: Developed in 1425

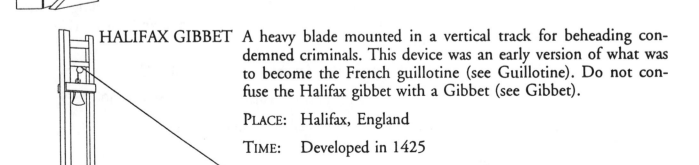

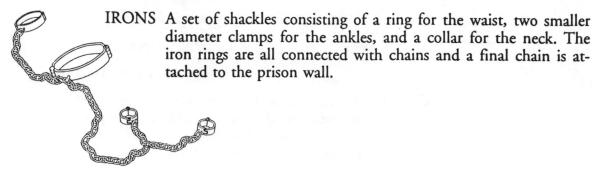

IRONS A set of shackles consisting of a ring for the waist, two smaller diameter clamps for the ankles, and a collar for the neck. The iron rings are all connected with chains and a final chain is attached to the prison wall.

JAGGS An iron collar that clamps around a prisoner's neck and chains him to the wall of a prison.

JOUGS An iron collar to chain a criminal to a wall or tree.

KNOUT A cruel whip made of several strands of interwoven thongs and wires mounted in a wooden handle. The strands are of uneven lengths. The longest strand can wrap around the body and whip the chest. The knout was an invention of the Russians and was first used to discipline their military. The whip was so vicious that it was quickly imported or copied to fill the needs of other European countries.

PLACE: Introduced in Russia

TIME: Mid-1600s

MAIDEN An execution machine with a heavy axe blade mounted in a vertical track. The maiden was designed by the Earl of Morton, regent of Scotland, after having seen the Halifax Gibbet (see Halifax Gibbet) in operation.

PLACE: Scotland

TIME: Mid-1500s

MANACLES A set of iron cuffs for restraining the hands. Crudely fashioned handcuffs.

PILLORY A device mounted on a pole at shoulder height with holes for the head and hands. A man or woman guilty of minor offenses such as drunkenness or laziness is locked in a standing position in the pillory for a day of public ridicule and abuse. (Compare with Stocks.)

PLACE AND TIME: Ancient Greece - 700 B.C.

Most villages of England - 1400s A.D.

Colonial America - 1500s

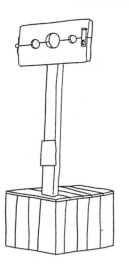

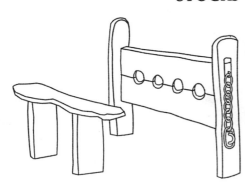

PLETI A whip consisting of three thongs of rawhide, each of which was tipped with a lead ball.

PLACE: Ancient Rome

TIME: 100 B.C.

SCEALDING STOOL A stool for confining and exposing female petty offenders to derision. (See Cucking Stool.)

SCOURGE Any whip used to punish people. An instrument for flogging.

SCUTICA A single-strand whip made of twisted and braided thongs of parchment leather.

STOCKS A device with holes for a person's legs and/or arms. A person guilty of a minor offense is locked in the stocks in a seated position and detained for a prescribed length of time. Paul and Silas (Acts 16:24) had their legs locked in stocks in the inner part of a Roman prison, not for public view but to ensure their confinement. Both the pillory and the stocks were adopted by the colonists in 16th century America.

PLACE AND TIME: Rome - 100 B.C.

England - 1400s

Colonial America - 1500s

WHIPPING POST A post set in a public place where those who commit petty offenses can be tied and whipped. The whipping post is frequently built as a part of a pillory or stocks. After whipping, the offender is locked in the stocks to think about it for a while.

PLACE: England and colonial America

TIME: 1400s

PART III: WARFARE

Armor

Weapons

Armor

EARLY ARMOR

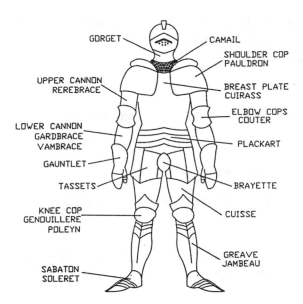

GORGET
CAMAIL
SHOULDER COP
PAULDRON
UPPER CANNON
REREBRACE
BREAST PLATE
CUIRASS
ELBOW COPS
COUTER
LOWER CANNON
GARDBRACE
VAMBRACE
PLACKART
GAUNTLET
TASSETS
BRAYETTE
KNEE COP
GENOUILLERE
POLEYN
CUISSE
SABATON
SOLERET
GREAVE
JAMBEAU

Armor is a defensive covering for the body, used by fighting men all around the world. At first, the protective coverings were made from animal skins, but leather, slats of bone, wood, scales, and rings of some hard material sewn to cloth or leather were soon used. Then, as metals became plentiful, the foot soldier was covered with armor made of steel or bronze.

PLACE AND TIME: Leather: Romans - 200 B.C.

Slats of bone: American Indians - pre-Colonial

Mail: Europe - 1000s to 1400s

Bronze and Steel: Europe - 1200s to 1600s

AILETTES Shoulder guards, worn with armor, but more for heraldic decoration than for protection. The ailette is the original form of the modern epaulet.

TIME: Late 1200s to mid 1300s

BISHOP'S MANTLE A tippet or shawl of mail covering the neck and shoulders. It was worn alone or over armor.

TIME: 1400s to mid 1500s

BRASSARD Armor for the entire arm. In more recent times, a brassard is an emblem or a badge worn on the arm to signify an office.

BRAYETTE An armored codpiece to protect the warrior's sex organs. Likely more decorative than functional.

BREAST PLATE Armor to protect the front of the body from the neck to the waist.

BRIGANDINE A coat of mail made of metal plates sewn to leather.

TIME: 1200s to 1500s

CAMAIL Armor for the neck and shoulders, consisting of interlocking chain mail fastened to the Basinet (see under Helmet) and providing a continuous covering from head to arms.

TIME: 1400s

CANNON   Armor for the arm. Upper cannon for the biceps, lower cannon for the forearm.

CORSELET   Armor for the body, consisting of steel or bronze plates or leather.

COUTER   Armor for the elbow (same as Elbow Cops).

CUIRASS   Armor consisting of a breastplate and backplate.

CUISSE   Armor for the thighs.

ELBOW COPS   Armor for the elbows.

GAMBESON   A coat made of leather or of cloth stuffed and quilted. It is sometimes worn under chain mail to pad the blows received. If worn alone, it is the sole armor.

GARDBRACE   Armor for the elbow (same as Elbow Cops).

GAUNTLET   Armor for the hand. Metal plates riveted to form a glove.

TIME: Early 1300s

GENOUILLERE   Armor for the knees (same as Knee Cops).

GORGET   Armor for the neck, first made of mail, later of metal plates.

TIME: 1400s

GREAVES   Armor for the lower leg. Roman and Greek greaves were made of either leather or bronze. Leather greaves continued to be used into the 14th century.

TIME: 300s to 1500s

HAUBERK   A full-length coat of mail covering the arms and long enough to reach the knees. The coat is split, allowing a knight to ride a horse.

TIME: 1000s to 1200s

JAMBEAU   Armor for the leg below the knee. (See Greaves.)

KNEE COPS   Armor for the kneecaps.

PAULDRON   Armor for the shoulder. (See Shoulder Cops.)

PLACKART   Armor for the stomach. The lower part of a breastplate.

POLEYN   Armor for the knees (same as Knee Cops).

TIME: 1300s

REREBRACE   Armor for the upper arm.

SABATON   A round-toed armored shoe. A form-fitting modification of solerets.

TIME: 1500s

SHOULDER COP Armor for the shoulder.

SOLERETS Plate armor for the feet.

TIME: 1200s

TASSETS Armor for the thighs, made of thin overlapping strips of metal riveted to straps. The tassets (or tacets) hung from the breastplate. Roman breastplates had leather tassets that hung in front of the tunic.

VAMBRACE Armor for the forearm.

HELMETS

Helmets are armor for the head. Helmet styles saw major changes during the Middle Ages. The soldier's helmet was changed as weapons and the techniques of using them changed. Change was not prompted as much by national uniformity, however, as by the metals available and the ingenuity of the iron craftsmen. An army from another country had no hesitation in adapting a new helmet if it fitted its needs. Dress armor for use in court was selected on the whims of fashion.

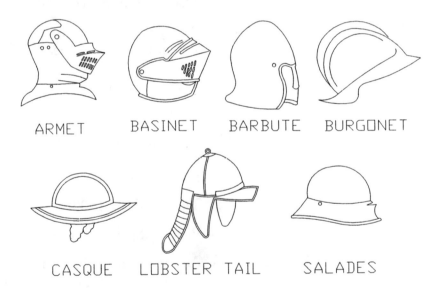

ARMET   BASINET   BARBUTE   BURGONET

CASQUE   LOBSTER TAIL   SALADES

ARMET A lightweight, form-fitting helmet that replaced the Basinet in the last part of the 15th century. The armet has a neckguard that transfers the weight of the helmet to the shoulders, making it more comfortable.

TIME: Late 1400s

BARBUTE Armor for the head. The helmet covers the head and neck with a face opening that yields a minimum of exposure.

TIME: 1400s

PLACE: Europe, especially Italy and Spain

BARREL HELM An early attempt at providing armor for the head. This helmet was awkward in that it hampered vision, impaired breathing, and was very heavy.

TIME: 1200s

BASINET   A helmet made of sheet steel, covering the head and neck to the shoulders. The helmet is equipped with a visor that hinges at the temples and is raised for comfort when the wearer is not engaged in battle. The visor can be completely detached by removing the hinge pins.

TIME: 1300s

PLACE: Europe, especially Germany and England

BEAVER   A section of helmet protecting the lower part of the face. The beaver evolved to become the movable face shield or visor.

BURGONET   A light open helmet of the 16th century. The identifying characteristic is a brim that projects over the eyes and another that protects the back of the neck. Most burgonets were elaborately decorated.

TIME: 1500s

PLACE: Europe, especially France and Italy

CABASSET   An open helmet worn by European foot soldiers. The name is Italian and means "pear." The identifying feature of the cabasset is a little point resembling a pear stem, projecting from the peak of the helmet.

TIME: Mid-1500s to early 1700s

CASQUE   A helmet combining the lines of a Burgonet (see Burgonet) and a classic Greek helmet. It is open-faced and frequently elaborately decorated.

TIME: Early 1500s

PLACE: Spain

CHAPEL DE FER   An iron hat with a crown and brim. This open helmet is lightweight and gives a wide field of vision, good for prolonged periods of fighting.

TIME: 1100s to 1400s

PLACE: Europe, especially France, Italy, and Switzerland

HEAUME   A heavy helmet that evolved from the barrel helm. Earflaps were added that join the Nasal (see Nasal), enclosing the face.

TIME: 1200s

LOBSTER TAIL   An open helmet with a guard at the back of the neck made of overlapping plates like a lobster's tail.

NASAL   The protective nosepiece of a helmet.

PANACHE A plume or bunch of feathers, worn as ornamentation on a helmet.

SALADE A helmet whose crown falls low on the face, covering eyes, nose, and ears. The brim flares at the bottom and is extended in a long sweep at the rear to protect the back of the neck.

TIME: 1400s

UMBREL The visor of a helmet that protects the face.

VISOR A movable face and eye shield that hinges to the helmet. Perforations in the face guard permit sight and speech.

BARDINGS

Bardings are armor for horses.

CHANFRON Armor for a horse's head.

CRINET Armor for the upper side of a horse's neck.

CRUPPER Armor for the hindquarters of a horse.

CUELLO Armor for the underside of a horse's neck.

FLANCHARD Armor for the sides of a horse.

PEYTRAL Armor for a horse's chest.

POITREL See Peytral.

SHABRACK A saddle cloth for a military horse.

TESTIERE Armor for a horse's head. (See Chanfron.)

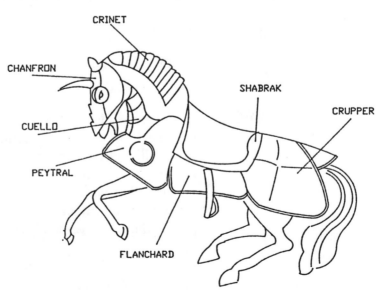

Weapons

FROM PREHISTORIC TIME

Man has felt the need for weapons from his earliest beginnings: the cave man found clubs to swing and stones to hurl. The flint blades and sharpened bones that were used to kill and skin animals were soon used on men. And although we do not know the weapon used, it is not likely that Cain killed Abel in a fistfight. Prehistoric men hunted with bows and arrows. As soon as men learned the rudiments of metallurgy they made swords. The tools a farmer used to till his soil were sometimes taken directly to the battlefield and used as tools of war to defend the land. Notable in this list are the axe, the pitchfork, the bill hook, and the threshing flail. All these implements evolved into dreadful weapons of their time.

BOWS AND ARROWS

The bow-and-arrow is used worldwide and comes to us from the earliest times. It is the oldest and most enduring weapon, remaining in use for long-range warfare until the 14th century, when it was replaced by handheld guns.

ARBALEST Any of several crossbows. (See Crossbow.)

PLACE: Europe

TIME: 500s A.D.

BLOWGUN A long tube of wood or cane through which arrows or darts are propelled by a man's breath. Although this weapon does not truly fall under the classification of archery, the blowgun shoots an arrow and can be lethal. The darts are very light and cannot be propelled with much force, so they are usually poisoned in order to make them effective. South American Indians use curare, a motor-nerve paralyzer poison related to strychnine.

SIZE: 6 to 10 feet long

PLACE: South America, particularly Brazil and Guiana; Malaya and Borneo

TIME: One of the earliest weapons to be developed

BOLT A dart to be shot from a crossbow. (See also Quarrel.)

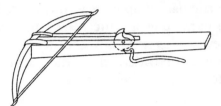

CROSSBOW An evolution of the bow-and-arrow. The bow is mounted crosswise to a grooved wooden stock, and the string is held and released mechanically. Some crossbows are so tightly strung that they must be drawn with a hand winch. (See Windlass Crossbow and Ballista.)

SIZE: Bow - 2½ feet long

PLACE: Europe, particularly Germany, Italy, and France

TIME: 1200 to 1400s

LONGBOW The weapon of the English foot soldier in the 14th century. The longbow is fully as long as the archer is tall and is proof that there are times when bigger can be better. It requires considerable strength and skill to fire the longbow with accuracy. It has about the same range as the crossbow, but it is much easier and faster to reload.

SIZE: 6 feet long

PLACE: England

TIME: 1300s

QUARREL A dart or an arrow with a four-edged head, used with a crossbow. (See also Bolt.)

QUIVER A case for carrying arrows.

SUMPITAN A blowpipe of Borneo.

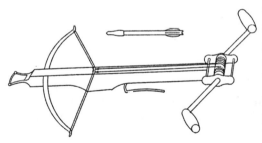

WINDLASS CROSSBOW A large crossbow, so tightly strung that a windlass winch is required to draw the string. This crossbow has great range but drawing the string takes precious time. The archer must set the front of the bow on the ground and place his foot in a stirrup to control the weapon's motions as he cranks the windlass. When the string is drawn and set into the trigger mechanism, the windlass is removed and the crossbow can be aimed and fired. The windlass was routinely used in conjunction with a Pavise (see under Shields) to protect the archer during this preparation time.

SIZE: Stock, from stirrup to windlass - 3½ feet long

PLACE: Europe

TIME: 1300s

GUNS

A gun is any weapon having a tube along which a projectile is propelled by means of an explosive force. The first guns were cannon. These evolved to a smaller, more portable weapon — the musket—that could be aimed and fired by one man. A still later development was the pistol, which could be managed with only one hand.

We usually know where a particular weapon was introduced, but it is sometimes difficult to name one specific *place* a firearm was used. They were all used everywhere. As any country introduced a new innovation using gunpowder, the other armies around the world were quick to add it to their arsenal.

ARQUEBUS   The arquebus was a handheld miniature version of the cannon. The first of these guns was heavy and needed to rest on a tripod when being aimed. The arquebus illustrated is from the 17th century.

PLACE: All of Europe

TIME: Introduced in the late 1300s

ARTILLERY   A gun too large to be managed by one man. Originally the term referred to the siege machines that threw stones (see Siege Machines).

BANDOLIER   A shoulder belt with pockets or loops for carrying ammunition. Bandoliers were in common use long before they became popular in the photos of Pancho Villa. When handguns were first introduced, the bandolier was developed to carry a handy supply of pre-measured charges of powder. It also often carried a priming charge and a bullet pouch.

PLACE: All of Europe, India, and the Orient

TIME: Late 1500s

BASILISK   Type of cannon (see chart).

BLUNDERBUSS   A short gun or pistol with a large bore used to scatter a load of shot at close range. Primarily used as protection against thieves. The blunderbuss was replaced by the shotgun in the early 19th century.

PLACE: Holland, England, and all of Europe

TIME: Early 1600s to 1800s

BOMBARD   Type of cannon (see chart).

BREECH LOADER   A firearm designed so the rear of the piece can be swung aside to load the missile and the charge into the barrel.

CANNON   The largest and earliest gun, consisting of a hollow cylinder from which projectiles are fired by means of explosives. From its introduction, the weapon showed great promise and within a period of fifty years the cannon replaced siege machines powerfully hurling large stones. Early in the 16th century cannon became lighter and more easily transported, and several sizes were in common use on the battlefield. Inventories of this period show eight to ten different cannon in the arsenals of both France and England. The cannon and the cannonball were in use as recently as the Civil War. In today's American army, a cannon is any gun with a bore greater than one inch.

PLACE: First made in Germany, spreading to all of Europe

TIME: Early 1300s

Cannon—14th to 16th Centuries			
	Size of gun bore (inches)	Weight of gun (pounds)	Weight of shot (pounds)
Dulle Guriete	—	—	700
Mons Meg	20.00	8000	350
Bombard	—	—	260
Cannon	8.00	8000	60
Curtald	—	3000	60
Bastard Cannon	7.00	4500	40
Culverin (snake)	5.50	4500	20
Basilisk (lizard)	5.00	4000	15
Demi Culverin	4.00	3400	10
Sacar (sparrow hawk)	3.50	1400	5
Minion (sweetheart)	3.50	1000	4
Falcon	2.50	660	2
Falconet	2.00	500	1.5

CARBINE A light gun, smaller than the musket and easier to maneuver, it soon became the horseman's gun. A semi-automatic .30 caliber rifle is now in use by the U.S. military and called by this same name.

PLACE: England

TIME: Late 1500s

CHAIN SHOT Ammunition for cannon consisting of two balls joined with a short length of chain. Primarily used to foul the sails and rigging of an enemy ship.

CULVERIN Type of cannon (see chart).

CURTALD Type of cannon (see chart).

DERRINGER A pistol small enough to hide in a pocket. The barrel was about an inch and a half long. The gun is named after its maker, Henry Derringer, but he designed and made many guns of all sizes.

SIZE: Barrel - 1½ inches long

PLACE: United States

TIME: 1855

DULLE GURIETE Type of cannon (see chart).

FALCON Type of cannon (see chart).

FLINTLOCK An improvement on the Wheel Lock (see Wheel Lock), using a piece of flint held in the hammer. When the hammer is released it forces the flint violently into a metal plate, and a shower of sparks is sent to the priming powder.

PLACE: Simultaneously introduced in Holland and Spain

TIME: Late 1500s

GUNPOWDER An explosive mixture of saltpeter, sulfur, and charcoal originally used by the Chinese in fireworks. The use of gunpowder for war rather than celebration was proposed by Roger Bacon in 1260. He thought it would make an effective bomb. The first time gunpowder was used for war was in a German cannon.

PLACE: Germany

TIME: 1326

HANDGUN The first handheld weapon using gunpowder was a simple tube attached to a long, straight handle. It was fired by means of a touch hole exactly like the full-sized guns. This gun was developed at the same time as the Arquebus (see Arquebus) and was in use in the late 14th century.

TIME: Late 1300s

HARQUEBUS An early portable firearm. (See Arquebus.)

LINSTOCK A forked staff holding a lighted match for firing a cannon.

PLACE: England

TIME: Mid-1500s

LIZARD Type of cannon (see chart).

MATCH A slow-burning cord or wick used to fire a cannon or Matchlock gun (see Matchlock).

MATCHLOCK An early mechanism for bringing match cord in contact with the priming charge of a gun, discharging it.

PLACE: Europe

TIME: 1400s

MINION Type of cannon (see chart).

MUSKET A portable infantry firearm. The earliest models were ignited with a Matchlock (see Matchlock) mechanism. Originally the musket was the largest gun that could be operated by one man, sometimes requiring a rest for firing. (See Arquebus.)

TIME: 1500s

MUZZLE LOADER A firearm that must be loaded from the front, through the barrel.

PARTRIDGE A large cannon or mortar used in sieges. The partridge mortar has multiple bores, the central barrel fires a standard cannon ball, and it is surrounded by several smaller ports that fire grenades.

TIME: 1400s

PETARD A heavy metal cone filled with explosives. The cone was fastened with its mouth to a wall or a gate. When the charge was exploded the cone directed the energy of the blast to the wall, forcing an opening.

PLACE: Europe

TIME: Late 1500s to 1600s

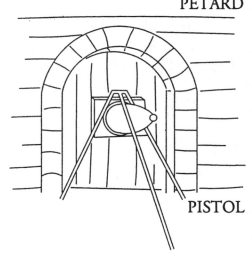

PISTOL A portable firearm small enough to be operated with one hand. The first pistol was fired with a Wheel Lock mechanism (see Wheel Lock).

PLACE: Introduced in France, quickly spreading to all Europe

TIME: Mid-1500s

SHRAPNEL An artillery shell filled with an explosive charge to spray bullets and jagged pieces of metal. This projectile was named after its inventor, British General Henry Shrapnel.

PLACE: England

TIME: 1800s

TOUCH HOLE The orifice in early cannons and portable firearms through which the powder was ignited.

WHEEL LOCK A mechanism to fire a gun that works much like a modern cigarette lighter. Flint or iron pyrites are touched to a spring-loaded revolving wheel. The resulting shower of sparks falls on the priming powder and fires the charge.

PLACE: Introduced in Germany

TIME: Early 1500s

── HAND WEAPONS ──

AXE A broad cutting blade mounted perpendicular to a short handle. One of the earliest weapons, brought directly from the farm to the battlefield.

BATTLE-AXE An axe designed especially for warfare. Many varieties were developed, some particularly effective against armor. In the 14th century the handle was lengthened to provide extra leverage. The battle-axe lost its distinction as the best offensive weapon against armor in the 17th century when improved firearms became plentiful.

SIZE: Blade 1¼ feet long; handle 3 to 4 feet long

PLACE: Europe and the Orient

TIME: 200 to 1700

BAGH NAKH An Eastern form of "brass knuckles." It is not used for punching, however, but for slashing. A crossbar with two rings is held in the palm of the hand, the forefinger and pinkie fitting through the rings. Four or five needle-sharp points are attached to the bar and project forward. The very descriptive English word for this weapon is "tiger's claw."

SIZE: Claws - 1 to 2 inches long

PLACE: India

TIME: 1600s to the present

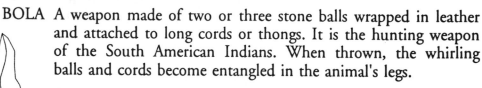

BIPENNIS An axe with a double-headed blade, one projecting on each side of the handle.

SIZE: 2 feet long

PLACE: Ancient Greece

TIME: 1000 to 800 B.C.

BOLA A weapon made of two or three stone balls wrapped in leather and attached to long cords or thongs. It is the hunting weapon of the South American Indians. When thrown, the whirling balls and cords become entangled in the animal's legs.

SIZE: Length of cords may vary from 2 feet to 3½ feet depending on size of prey

PLACE: Argentina - (plains Indians)

Alaska - (Eskimos)

TIME: Pre-colonial to the present

BOOMERANG A flat, curved wooden missile thrown for hunting or warfare. Only a few boomerangs are designed to return to the thrower if the target is missed.

SIZE: 2 to 2½ feet long

PLACE: Egypt, Africa, India, Australia (aborigines)

TIME: 2000 B.C. to the present

BRASS KNUCKLES An iron or brass covering for the knuckles of a fist. Adds weight and effect to the punch in rough street fighting. Brass knuckles are a refinement of the Cestus (see Cestus) used in first century Rome.

SIZE: Sized to fit a man's fist

PLACE: Europe and United States

TIME: Evolved from Rome 100 A.D. to the present

CESTUS A leather band worn on the hands of boxers. Often loaded with lead or other metal to give greater effect to the blows.

PLACE: Rome

TIME: 100 A.D.

FLAIL A free-swinging bar attached to a wooden handle. Originally an instrument for threshing grain by hand, the flail was taken from the farm to the battlefield. As a weapon, it was fitted with chains, weights, and/or spikes.

SIZE: Handle - 1½ to 2½ feet long; swinging bar - about ¾ of handle length

PLACE: Europe and Asia

TIME: 500 to 1800

MACE A heavy war club with metal spikes or flanges radiating from the head. The mace was used in hand-to-hand battles against armored warriors.

SIZE: 2½ to 3½ feet long

PLACE: Italy, Germany, Poland, England, Persia, Turkey, China, Japan

TIME: 1000 to 1600

MARTEL-DE-FER A hammer of iron used to pierce and break armor. The head of the weapon has a hammer on one side and a pick on the other.

SIZE: 3 to 4 feet long

PLACE: Europe and Asia

TIME: 1000 to 1600

MORNING STAR A heavy spiked ball attached to the chains of a flail (see Flail).

> SIZE: Handle - 3 feet long; chain - 1 foot long; ball - 3 inches in diameter
>
> PLACE: Europe
>
> TIME: 1000 to 1600

SLING A strip of leather or some other flexible material with a pocket near the center for holding a missile. The sling is swung rapidly, one end of the strip is released, and the missile is projected by centrifugal force. A sling is sometimes mounted on a pole, the longer length increasing the range of the weapon.

> SIZE: From end of strip to pocket - 3 feet long
>
> PLACE: Worldwide
>
> TIME: From earliest times

TOMAHAWK A light axe used as a tool and a weapon. The earliest axes were fitted with a stone or bone head, but in the 15th century the stone head gave way to iron.

> SIZE: Handle - 2 feet long; head - 10 inches wide
>
> PLACE: North America (Algonquian Indians)
>
> TIME: Early times to the present

TRUNCHEON A short heavy stick or club. Modern usage refers to a policeman's nightstick.

--- **KNIVES** ---

A knife is a small handheld cutting or thrusting weapon. There is no clear-cut identifying feature that distinguishes a knife from a dagger, a machete, a saber, or a sword. Although the terms are useful for distinguishing the weapon types, there is much overlap in meaning. Neither length of blade, kind of hilt, nor method of use can clearly and absolutely define the various weapons.

BALISONG A knife with a split handle that folds around both sides of the blade, completely enclosing it. The unique handle design allows for some flashy flourishes in the hands of one who knows how to use it.

> SIZE: Blade - 4 to 6 inches long

PLACE: Philippine Islands

BODKIN — Any small dagger with a slender blade. A stiletto.

BOWIE KNIFE — A strong single-edged hunting knife. Reputedly invented by James Bowie. (Compare with Scramasax.)

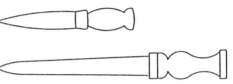

SIZE: Blade - 8 to 10 inches long

PLACE: United States

TIME: Early 1800s to the present

CLASP KNIFE — Any knife with a blade that folds into the handle.

DAGGER — Any short, sharp-edged, pointed stabbing weapon that does not have a folding blade.

DIRK — A dagger with a single-edged blade that tapers uniformly from the handle to the point. The grip is barrel-shaped and has no pommel.

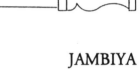

SIZE: Blade - 6 to 12 inches long

PLACE: Scotland (Highlanders)

TIME: 1700 to 1800

JAMBIYA — A knife with a double-edged curved blade. The distinguishing features of this knife are the curved blade and the handle with a short grip and large pommel. The jambiya was one of the first items made when the Iron Age began in Arabia.

SIZE: Blade - 10 to 16 inches

PLACE: Arabia

TIME: 1000 B.C.

KATAR — A double-edged knife with a unique handle design. The handle is made of two parallel bars that run in the same plane to the blade. The bars are reinforced and kept parallel by two (or more) crossbars. The proportions of the knife blade are also distinctive; it is unusually wide for its length. The blade may be 1½ inches wide where it joins the handle, then it tapers to a point in as little as 6 inches. A longer sword version of this knife is called a Pata. The blade proportions described above, of course, do not apply to the sword version.

SIZE: Blade - 6 to 36 inches long

PLACE: India

TIME: Very ancient, dating back to the earliest of times

KRISSES — A Malay dagger with a wavy-edged blade. The handle is usually made of wood, bone, ivory, or horn and carved in the figure of a bird, an animal, a snake, or a demon.

SIZE: Blade - 6 to 24 inches long

PLACE: Indonesia

TIME: 1300s

MAIN GAUCHE A dagger used in fencing. It is held in the left hand and used as a guard, the fencing sword being wielded in the right.

SIZE: Blade - 16 inches long

PLACE: Europe, especially Spain and Italy

TIME: 1600s

POCKET KNIFE A knife having one or more blades that fold into the handle.

PONIARD A stiletto, usually with a slender triangular or square blade.

SIZE: Blade - 14 inches long

PLACE: Europe

TIME: Mid-1500s

QUILLON DAGGER A left-handed knife used as a companion to the rapier, which is held in a fighter's right hand.

SIZE: Blade - 16 inches long

PLACE: Europe

TIME: 1600s

RONDEL DAGGER A dagger with a blade that is triangular in cross-section and is durable enough to find chinks in armor without breaking. The handle is designed to be used in an overhand stab.

SIZE: Blade - 12 inches long

PLACE: Europe

TIME: 1400s

SCRAMASAX A single-edged dagger that looks like an oversized hunting knife and is variously used as a weapon and a machete.

SIZE: Blade - 12 to 16 inches long

PLACE: Western and Central Europe

TIME: 600s to 800s

STILETTO Any dagger with a very slender blade that tapers uniformly from the hilt to the tip.

SIZE: Blade - 6 to 10 inches long

PLACE: Europe and United States

TIME: 1500s to the present

SWITCHBLADE A pocket knife with a spring-operated blade that is released by pressing a button on the handle.

SIZE: Blade - 5 inches long

PLACE: Central America and Mexico

TIME: 1900s

—— POLEARMS ——

A polearm is any cutting or thrusting blade or axe head that has been fitted on a long pole or handle.

AWL PIKE   A pike with a long, slim, straight head, shaped like a needle.

SIZE: 9 to 10 feet long

PLACE: Germany, Austria, Switzerland

TIME: 1400s

ASSEGAI   A javelin or throwing spear. The spear head is leaf-shaped and usually made of iron.

SIZE: 4½ to 5 feet long

PLACE: South Africa (Kaffirs and Swazi tribesmen)

BERDICHE   A poleaxe with a long, narrow, curved axe head. The blade extends beyond the shaft far enough so the weapon can be used for thrusting.

SIZE: 8 feet long

PLACE: Germany, Poland, Russia, Turkey

TIME: 1400 to 1600

BILL   A halberd with a broad hook-shaped blade. The design of this weapon evolved from a peasant's pruning tool called a billhook and became the characteristic weapon of the English infantry in medieval times.

SIZE: 9 feet long

PLACE: England

TIME: 1300 to 1600

BOAR SPEAR   A hunting spear with a broad leaf-shaped head. Early in the 16th century these spears were used in battle by the yeomen of Henry VIII.

SIZE: 7½ feet long

PLACE: Africa and England

TIME: 1500s

GLAIVE   A stout single-edged sword blade mounted on a long staff, suitable for both cutting and thrusting. (Also a broadsword.)

SIZE: 8½ feet long

PLACE: Europe and China

TIME: 1400 to 1500

HALBERD   A polearm that combines the spear and battle-axe. The blade, shaped like a cleaver, is effective against armor. The halberd always has a stout spike projecting at the tip for thrusting and a secondary spike or hook on the rear of the head used for grappling.

SIZE: 8½ feet long

PLACE: England

TIME: 1400 to 1600

JAVELIN   A lightweight spear for throwing. The javelin has a wooden shaft and an iron point. It is used for hunting, for war, and for long-distance throwing contests. (See also Assegai.)

SIZE: 3 to 4 feet long

PLACE: Africa, Europe, the Orient

TIME: Earliest times to the present

KORSEKE   A three-bladed polearm. The center blade is 12 to 14 inches long and sharply pointed. Two shorter blades are forged to the base of the main blade on either side and at acute angles to it.

SIZE: 7½ feet long

PLACE: Italy

TIME: 1400 to 1500

LANCE   A thrusting spear used by mounted soldiers. The shaft is cylindrical for almost the entire length and about 2 inches in diameter.

SIZE: 12 to 14 feet long

PLACE: Europe, particularly England

TIME: 700s

LINSTOCK   A pike (sometimes with a spearhead) having an attachment to hold a lighted match for firing cannon.

SIZE: 4 feet long

PLACE: Europe

TIME: 1550s

LOCHABER AXE   A polearm consisting of a short, stout thrusting blade and a sharp grappling hook mounted on a staff. The lochaber evolved from the Glaive (see Glaive).

SIZE: 8½ feet long

PLACE: Scotland

TIME: 1500s

PARTISAN   A weapon carried by the king's guard. This thrusting spear's head resembled the blade of a broadsword with curved hooks at the base. It was elaborately engraved and largely ceremonial. The soldier's weapon of the same basic design is called a Korseke (see Korseke).

SIZE: 6 feet long

PLACE: Europe

TIME: 1500 to 1600

PIKE   A long pole having a metal spearhead, used by foot soldiers in medieval warfare.

SIZE: 7 feet long

PLACE: Europe, especially Rome

TIME: 300 B.C. to 1500 A.D.

PILUM   A heavy pike or throwing spear used by infantrymen.

SIZE: 7 feet long

PLACE: Rome (Legionaries)

TIME: 100 B.C.

POLEAXE   An offshoot of the battle-axe, the axe head is mounted on a long shaft. A hammer head may be mounted on the reverse side of the axe blade.

SIZE: 6 to 7 feet long

PLACE: Europe

TIME: 1000 to 1500

RAVENSBILL   See Poleaxe.

SPEAR Any shafted weapon with a sharp point intended for thrusting or throwing.

SPONTOON A short Partisan (see Partisan) primarily used for ceremony. Officers in the British army used the spontoon for signaling orders to their soldiers in the field.

SIZE: 4½ feet long

PLACE: England

TIME: 1600 to 1700

TRIDENT A three-pronged spear used in gladiatorial fights. A similar weapon was in common use by many countries in the Orient.

SIZE: 5 feet long

PLACE: Rome

TIME: 100 A.D.

VOULGE A cleaver-shaped knife blade mounted on a long pole. It was a forerunner of the Halberd (see Halberd).

SIZE: 8 feet long

PLACE: Europe, particularly France

TIME: 1200 to 1300

SHIELDS

BUCKLER A small round shield, with a knob projecting from the center. The buckler is commonly carried on an archer's belt alongside his short sword to be used when the enemy comes into hand-to-hand combat range.

SIZE: 16 to 18 inches in diameter

PLACE: England

TIME: 1200s to 1400s

CETRA A circular Roman shield.

SIZE: 3 feet in diameter

PLACE: Rome

TIME: 100 A.D.

MANTELET A transportable shelter used to shield the attackers during a particular phase of a siege. It sometimes houses a battering ram and its crew. (See Battering Ram.) A more modern use of the word describes the bulletproof shield around an artillery gun to protect the gun crew.

PAVISE A rectangular man-sized shield. It can be propped against poles that hinge from the rear, and provides cover for an archer's whole body.

SIZE: 4 feet wide, 6 feet tall

PLACE: Italy

TIME: 1400s to 1500s

SCUTUM A long leather-covered wooden shield used by the infantrymen of the Roman Legions.

SIZE: 26 inches wide, 36 inches tall

PLACE: Rome

TIME: 100 A.D.

A body of Roman soldiers could interweave their shields above their heads and provide a protective covering called a testudo. Such a shield was used to give an attacking siege team some protection from the hail of missiles thrown down from the castle walls.

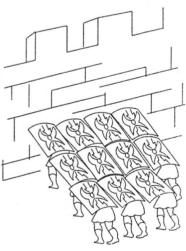

TARGET A round Buckler (see Buckler) made of leather-covered wood. The shield is covered with many small brass studs in geometric patterns. The central knob is frequently spiked, and the small maneuverable shield can be used offensively.

SIZE: 20 to 24 inch diameter

PLACE: Scotland

TIME: 1100 to 1300s

TARIAN   A bronze Buckler (see Buckler) used by the tribal nations settling in early England. When hit with a sword, these metal shields could be heard for a great distance.

SIZE: 20 inch diameter

PLACE: Britain

TIME: 500s

SIEGE MACHINES

A siege machine is a large apparatus or engine for storming a castle or walled fortress. Some machines were designed to break down the walls; others were launchers for throwing stones, arrows, fire pots, and other missiles at the defenders. Attackers built these oversized devices on the battlefield as soon as the castle was cut off from outside assistance. The siege machine had its beginning in the period of the Roman conquests, and its use continued until the 16th century when a cannon could destroy a wall with greater efficiency.

BALLISTA   A projectile-throwing engine built along the concept of the crossbow. One of the smaller of these engines, the ballista can be operated by two men and is used for throwing large arrows or stone balls.

PLACE AND TIME: Rome - 300s

Europe - 1100s to 1500s

BATTERING RAM   A long heavy beam with an iron head, used to penetrate a door or a stone wall. The simplest ram is carried by a number of men and repeatedly smashed against a wall. A more efficient ram swings on ropes from an overhead frame. The framework is equipped with a roof to protect the several men necessary to operate the assault weapon from the defenders stationed at the top of the wall.

PLACE: Europe

TIME: 1100s to late 1300s

BELFRY A three- or four-story tower, mounted on wheels, used to assault a walled fortification. A team of men and horses pull and push the tower from its battlefield construction site to the wall. Archers on the top level attempt to clear the wall of its defenders while a drawbridge is set in place, allowing assault troops on a lower level to cross over.

PLACE: Europe

TIME: 1100s to 1300s

CATAPULT An engine for throwing stones. The throwing arm is powered by a tightly twisted skein of cord or sinew. When the catapult arm is suddenly released, the missile is flung toward enemy lines.

PLACE: Europe

TIME: 1100s to 1500s

FUSEE A rocket directed toward a wall of a fort under siege to set it on fire. The fusee, a product of early gunpowder technology, was a transition piece between the siege machine and the cannon.

PLACE: Europe

TIME: 1300s

MANGONEL A general term to cover machines that throw large stones and clay pots filled with burning materials.

ONAGER An early Roman version of the Catapult (see Catapult).

PLACE: Rome

TIME: 300s

TREBUCHET   A medieval catapult for throwing heavy missiles. The trebuchet was powered by a heavy weight hung from a pivoted beam. The missile was thrown by a sling attached to the other, much longer, end of the beam.

PLACE: Europe

TIME: 1100s to 1500s

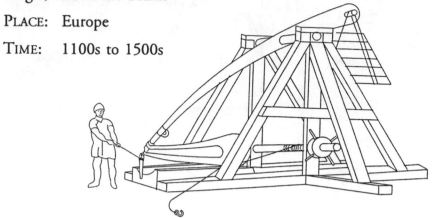

———— SWORDS ————

The sword replaced the club as soon as man discovered how to use metals. The swords used by Jacob's sons Simeon and Levi (Genesis 34:25) were most likely made of bronze. The tooling of iron was developed in Asia Minor in about 1100 B.C., and very soon the craftsmen of Asia, Africa, and Europe all began making swords.

Each nation or clan of fighters had their own idea of how to handle a sword and what it should do. Most swords were designed for both cutting and thrusting, but many were specifically fashioned to be superior at a single assignment. Swords have always been designed to fill the needs of the fighting styles of the men who developed them.

The sword of the modern day soldier is the fixed bayonet. Motion picture producers are still designing fantasy swords to fill the needs of fantasy characters of fantasy lands.

ANLACE   A short broad sword. (See Cinquedea.)

BADELAIRE   A sword with a short, broad, curved blade. The feature that distinguishes this sword from other falchion blades is the large "S"-shaped hand guard.

SIZE: Blade - 28 inches long

PLACE: Europe

TIME: 1500s

BALDRIC   A harness designed to allow a nobleman to wear his rapier or sabre.

It consists of a looped belt that passes from a shoulder to the opposite hip. The sword is attached to the strap at the waist.

BROADSWORD A classification used to describe any sword with a wide, straight, double-edged blade.

SIZE: Blade - 36 to 38 inches long

PLACE AND TIME: Rome - 100s

Elsewhere in Europe - 1200s to 1500s

CANNELURE A groove cut into the length of a sword to lighten the blade without lessening its strength. The Japanese call these channels "blood grooves."

CINQUEDEA A short broadsword. It is double-edged and tapers from the hilt to the point.

SIZE: Blade - 20 to 24 inches long, 3 inches wide at the hilt

PLACE: Europe, particularly Italy

TIME: 1400s

CLAYMORE A double-edged broad sword weighing about 5 pounds and requiring the use of both hands to wield.

SIZE: Blade - 42 inches long; hilt - 14 inches long

PLACE: Scotland

TIME: Mid-1500s

CUTLASS A short, single-edged, slightly curved sword. It is the saber preferred by sailors.

SIZE: Blade - 24 inches long

PLACE: Europe, and the high seas

TIME: 1700s

EPÉE A dueling sword designed for thrusting. It has a lightweight flexible blade with a triangular or quadrilateral cross-section and a sharp point.

SIZE: Blade - 32 inches long

PLACE: Europe

TIME: 1600s to 1700s

FALCHION A broad, short, single-edged cutting sword with a slightly curved blade. The blade is widest near the point, and the back meets the tip of the cutting edge in a concave curve.

SIZE: Blade - 28 inches long

PLACE: Europe

TIME: 1300s

FOIL   A blunted blade used in the sport of fencing. It has a lightweight square blade, ending with a button on the tip.

SIZE: Blade - 32 inches long

PLACE: Europe and United States

TIME: 1800s

GLADIUS   A Roman short sword used for close combat.

SIZE: Blade - 20 inches long, 2 inches wide

PLACE: Rome (Legionaries)

TIME: 100 A.D.

HANGER   Any light saber that hangs from the belt. This sword and its harness were popular with court noblemen and became an accepted part of their attire.

PLACE: Europe

TIME: 1600s to 1700s

KATANA   The primary sword of the samurai warrior. The straight blade is single-edged. The hilt is large and can be wielded with one or both hands. It is covered with sharkskin and wound with cord or flat braid.

SIZE: Blade - 21 inches long; hilt - 10 inches long

PLACE: Japan

TIME: 1200s to 1860s

MACHETE   A long, heavy, broad-bladed knife or cutlass. It is used in Central and South America as both tool and weapon.

SIZE: Blade - 20 inches long

PLACE: Central and South America

TIME: 1600s to the present

MISERICORD   A slender sword used to deliver the death wound (coup de grace) to an injured knight.

PATA   A longer version of the dagger of India. (See Katar.)

RAPIER A narrow, straight-bladed court sword. The design evolved through the years as the techniques of using the sword developed. At first it was double-edged and could be used for cutting and thrusting. In the 17th century, as the art of fencing developed among the nobility, the rapier was modified and used solely for thrusting.

SIZE: Blade - 32 to 38 inches long

PLACE: Spain, France, and England

TIME: 1500s to 1700s

SABER Any sword that is single-edged and has a slightly curved blade with uniform width. It is intended for cutting but can also be effective for thrusting. The saber is still worn as a dress sword by the U.S. Marines.

SIZE: Blade - 34 to 36 inches long

PLACE: Europe and United States (cavalry officers)

TIME: 1800 to 1900s

SAMURAI SWORD The sword of the feudal Japanese warrior. Three swords make up the set of samurai weapons: the katana, the wakizashi, and the tanto. Feudalism ended officially in 1867, but the ceremonial swords have continued to the present day. (See separate entries for each sword).

PLACE: Japan

TIME: 1200 to 1860s

SCIMITAR Any saber with an exaggerated curve in the blade.

SIZE: Blade - 28 to 34 inches long

PLACE: Turkey, Persia, Arab nations

SHAMSHIR A saber with an exaggerated curve. The blade has too much curve to be effective in thrusting, so it is used strictly as a slashing weapon. (See Scimitar.)

SIZE: Blade - 28 to 32 inches long

PLACE: Persia, Turkey, India

SHORT SWORD Any broad double-edged sword less than 24 inches long.

TANTO A dagger in the family of samurai swords. The design parallels that of the katana and the wakizashi.

SIZE: Blade - 10 inches long; hilt - 5 inches long

PLACE: Japan

TIME: 1200 to 1860s

WAKIZASHI The short sword of the samurai warrior. It is identical in every way to the katana except for its shorter length. This sword is worn and used in conjunction with the katana. It is also the sword used for ceremonial suicide—*hara-kiri.*

Blade: 13 inches long

PLACE: Feudal Japan

TIME: 1200s to 1860s

XIPHOS GLADIUS A short Roman sword used in close combat. (See Gladius.)

SIZE: Blade - 20 inches long

PLACE: Rome

TIME: 100 A.D.

PART IV: SCIENCE AND TECHNOLOGY

Stone Age Tools
Alchemy
Dowsing
Telephones

Stone Age Tools

— PRIMITIVE TOOLS —

Primitive man around the entire world made and used stone weapons for his defense and flint tools for his everyday needs. During the Stone Age, tools were made of many natural materials, including bone, flint, polished stone, hard wood, ivory, and jade. These implements remained in use long after 3000 B.C. when bronze was invented, or even 1000 B.C. when iron was introduced.

Old ways die hard, perhaps the newer metals were profane, or perhaps it was tradition, but flint knives were used for ceremonial purposes well into the periods of recorded history when better tools were available. The Egyptians used flint knives in embalming their dead. The priests of Mexico used stone knives to remove the hearts of sacrificial victims.

The drawings on this page represent tools found in the ancient flint beds of England. They date to antiquity.

AXE HEAD This axe head is fitted to a split branch handle and lashed firmly in place with thongs made of deerskin. The axe could be used either as a weapon to make war or as a tool to shape wood and strip the bark from logs.

SIZE: 6 inches long, 1 inch thick; weight, 3 pounds

KNIFE The flint knife is frequently sharpened on both edges. The curved edge of this knife allows the chisel edge to be pulled toward the operator as he slices away shavings. The butt end of the blade is polished smooth for a good hand hold.

SIZE: 4 inches long

PICK HEAD The triangular pick head is used in hollowing out tree log canoes. Both ends of the cutting head are available once it is set into a handle. The log is set on fire and the charred wood is chipped away with the sharp flint blades.

SIZE: 4 inches long, 3 inches wide

PUNCH   A slender flint pick is used to punch and saw holes into tough animal skins. It may also be repeatedly twisted in wood to drill holes.

SIZE: 4 inches long, ³/₄ inch thick

SAW   A flint saw is used with equal effect on soft wood or tough animal skins.

SIZE: 5 inches wide

SCRAPER   Scraping blades are made in several styles for the different operations involved in skinning an animal and in cleaning the pelt. A curved blade is good for making incisions and doing the initial skinning. The disc scraper is for removing fat and hair.

SIZE: 4 inches wide

Alchemy

EARLY CHEMISTRY

Alchemy is the forerunner of chemistry. Europeans learned the basic concepts of alchemy from the Arabs during the Crusades and developed techniques of manipulating mineral compounds and procedures that are still in use by chemists today. The primary objective of alchemy is the search for the Philosopher's Stone: the formula for transmuting common metals into gold.

The alchemist knew early on that he could remove contaminants from a liquid by careful distillation. He was certain that the same process could be used to purify common metals, producing gold. Applying the principle of distillation to solid minerals, a process called *sublimation* and an apparatus called *aludels* were developed. Distillation and sublimation were powerful tools of the alchemist. Some very pure minerals (sulfur for instance) were developed, and although some experimenters claimed success in producing gold, nobody got rich.

Experiments were shrouded in secrecy. Formulas were written with symbols. Many code words and drawings had cryptic meanings and were thoroughly understood only by the initiated. Critical processes, however, were carefully ciphered to have meaning only to the one taking the notes.

The definitions of items found in this section sometimes rely on each other for clarity. For instance, you will not fully understand what a Pelican is without cross-referencing to learn the meaning of Alembic and Cucurbite, as the individual entries suggest.

All the equipment used in the alchemy labratory can be dated 1100 to 1700.

ADOPTER A round-bodied vessel with a narrow neck and a beaked spout on one side. The adopter can be placed between the head and receiver of an alembic (see Alembic) as a second condenser.

ALEMBIC A multi-part apparatus made of metal or glass for distilling liquids. The unit consists of a bulbous body with a long neck called a "cucurbite" (see Cucurbite). This part contains the liquid and, when set on a stove, it allows the temperature of the solution to be raised to a controlled boil. The top unit is the "head," a condenser that turns the vapors to a distilled liquid. The third part is called a "receiver." It is a reservoir to store the collected distillate.

SIZE: 1½ to 3 feet high

ALKAHEST A long-time quest of the alchemist—the universal solvent.

ALUDELS A column of pear-shaped vessels used to purify solids through sublimation. The bottom vessel, the cucurbite (see Cucurbite), contains the mineral to be purified and is heated over a stove. The glasses in the middle of the stack have open tops and bottoms, allowing them to be fitted into a tall column. This stack of containers acts as a condenser. As the heated vapors cool, the purified mineral collects on the sides of the individual globes as a powder. The top aludel (called a head) is equipped with a long beak and is open only at the bottom. It is the coolest part of the condenser and collects most of the powder.

SIZE: The height of the aludels depends on the size of the individual units and the number of units installed in the column. Smaller units can be assembled on a workbench. Other applications call for a stack as tall as a man and have to be erected from the floor of the laboratory.

ATHANOR A reverberating furnace designed to raise the temperature of an object slowly and then maintain an almost constant heat. It is a specialized form of kiln (see Kiln). The athanor was a necessary heat source as the alchemist attempted to "hatch" the philosophical egg (see Philosophical Egg).

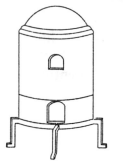

SIZE: Furnaces were made in a great number of sizes. Some were like our modern hibachi; others were the size of a blacksmith's furnace, taking up a whole room.

BALANCE A simple device for accurately measuring small quantities of weight. Two dishes of equal mass hang from a crossbeam. The beam is supported at its precise center. A sample of unknown weight is placed in one dish and the other dish is loaded with a ballast of known weights until the balance beam is level.

SIZE: 1 to 2 feet high

BALLOON A short-necked round-bottomed flask. This piece of glassware is frequently used as a receiver in an alembic. (See Alembic.)

SIZE: 6 to 18 inches high

BELL A large glass cover in the shape of a bell. The bell was placed over a reactant to separate it from the immediate environment and to control its surrounding atmosphere. Many of the alchemist's operations needed to be performed in a humid atmosphere.

SIZE: 1½ to 2 feet in diameter

BUDDLING DISH A flat pan or shallow trough for washing mineral ores.

COUPEL A metallic dish for testing precious metals.

SIZE: 2 to 20 inches in diameter

CRUCIBLE A pot, hardened to withstand extreme heat, for holding molten metals. The "Hessian crucible," from Hess, Germany, was made of native clay and fine sand tempered to withstand sudden changes in temperature. The crucible held liquified ore till the impurities were boiled out and the dross could be skimmed from the surface.

CUCURBITE A gourd-shaped vessel used to contain a liquid and heat it to a controlled boil. One form of cucurbite is the Matrass (see Matrass).

FURNACE Any stove, oven, or kiln used to heat an alchemist's compounds and solutions. The furnace is fueled with animal oils, wood, coal, or charcoal and frequently fanned with a large bellows.

GALLEY A type of furnace in which several vessels are heated at the same time, lined up side by side.

KILN A furnace or an oven used to heat an object for the purpose of drying, hardening, or baking. The oven is designed to heat slowly, hold an even heat for a long period, and cool slowly.

LUTE Any putty or cement used to seal the union between two glass containers. A flexible putty is made by mixing clay and linseed oil. The lute could be made of beeswax or resins. A more rigid connection was made by soaking a linen ribbon in quicklime and egg white and wrapping the joint with this strip.

MATRASS
A bulbous bottle with a long neck. The matrass was frequently used as a cucurbite.

SIZE: 6 to 20 inches in diameter

MORTAR
A very hard stone or metal bowl in which softer materials are hammered or ground to a powder. It is almost always associated with a pestle (see Pestle).

SIZE: 4 to 8 inches high

PELICAN
A specialized form of alembic. This apparatus recirculates the distillate back into the base, to be revaporized and condensed in a cyclic process.

SIZE: 1 to 3 feet high

PESTLE
An instrument to be used with a mortar for grinding and crushing solid materials to powder. (See Mortar.)

PHILOSOPHICAL EGG
A final step in the search for the philosopher's stone. The egg is a round-bottomed crystal container holding a brine solution (rebus). The end of the glass container is sealed, and the unit is heated in an oven in the hope that the fertilized egg will hatch and become the philosopher's stone.

REBUS
A solution of metals, salts, acids, and crystals formulated in the process of searching for the philosopher's stone.

RETORT
A single piece of glassware to be used in distilling less volatile liquids. The retort has a round or teardrop-shaped body and an extended beak, which acts as a condenser.

SIZE: 4 to 12 inches in diameter

SCALE
A device for measuring small quantities of weight. (See Balance.)

VESSEL
Any container to hold the chemicals that are being tested or exposed to reactions. Glass, metal, and earthenware receptacles are common.

Glass
Although glass was expensive and sometimes broke under the extreme temperatures required of many experiments, it was unaffected by acid and did not enter into the reactions. It was

preferred by most alchemists.

Metal Metallic vessels were best for high heat, but they sometimes entered into and contaminated any procedure that involved acids.

Earthenware Pottery was porous and frequently trapped reactants, contaminating the vessel and making it useless for future experiments.

Dowsing

HISTORY

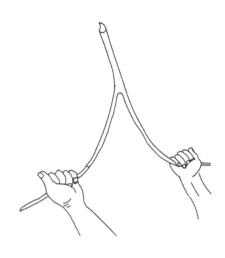

For many centuries magicians, foretellers, and prophets have used rods or wands in their divinations to interpret the will of the gods and to indicate a course of action. However, it seems that dowsing—the practice of using a forked tree branch to find underground minerals—is unknown in classical times.

Dowsing began about 450 years ago in Germany, coming out of the search for metal ore. Georgius Agricola recorded his observations at a mining camp. Quotation marks appear on the following statement, but it is really an edited paraphrase of a translation of his report. "The dowsers hold their closed fists horizontal, with their fingers turned up grasping a forked twig with the main trunk of the branch pointed skyward. They wander at random through the hilly region. At the moment they walk across a vein, the branch suddenly turns and twists, dipping down to the earth, pointing to the place to dig."

PLACE: Germany

TIME: 1556

The practice of dowsing for minerals, and then for water, spread throughout Europe. The English, French, Dutch, Spanish, and Portuguese brought the techniques into the United States, Canada, and Mexico. Some American Indians have been highly successful at water witching, but the practice was unknown in America until it was introduced by Europeans. The dowser in England is known as a "jawser"; in France he is called a "sourcier"; at work in rural parts of the United States today, he prefers to be called a "water witch."

Along with the traditional method, several spinoff techniques have been developed by some dowsers. Many objects have been used as divining rods, including candle snuffers, scissors, bucket handles, smoked sausages, and the open hands.

BAGUETTE A stick used as a divining rod. The baguette has a slight bend in its length. It is balanced on the index fingers of each hand as the hands are outstretched vertically and held waist high. The baguette begins to rock or swing as the dowser passes over an underground water source.

PLACE: France

TIME: 1600s to 1700s

DIVINING ROD   A forked branch or other object in the hands of a dowser who is in search of underground water.

FORKED TWIG   A forked branch, cut from a hazel bush, is considered by most dowsers to be the orthodox divining rod. However, it is true that others have been equally successful with a branch from a peach, a persimmon, a willow, or an apple tree.

SIZE: 18 inches long

PLACE AND TIME: France - late 1600s

England and United States - late 1700s to the present

PENDULE EXPLORATEUR   A ring attached to a handheld thread. When a lost or hidden thing is within range of the pendulum its presence is indicated by either a swing or a rotation of the ring.

SIZE: 18 inches from fingertips to ring

PLACE: Europe and United States

TIME: 1800s to the present

PLANCHETTE   A triangular board, supported by three legs, which holds a pencil or pointer. It is believed by some that the planchette can spell out messages when a person rests his fingers lightly on the board's surface.

SWIVELING RODS   A recent addition to the family of dowsing indicators, a pair of "L"-shaped metal rods, one held in each fist of the dowser. The rods swivel toward each other and even cross forming an "X" when the dowser walks over a water source. Bent wires made from a coat hanger work as well.

SIZE: 14 inches long

PLACE: United States

TIME: 1800s

Telephones

EARLY INNOVATION

The telephone found worldwide acceptance as soon as it was invented. The entries and illustrations that follow are descriptive of the Bell Telephone System in the United States. Simultaneous progress was being made in the major cities in Europe, notably Paris and London.

The date listed with each entry below indicates the time an innovation was first introduced. Once a piece of equipment was installed, it tended to remain in use for a long time. The telephone was ruggedly made, and engineers were careful that new models did not make older installations out of date. "Hello, Central" phones continued to operate on the same lines with dial phones until they could be replaced. When the touch-tone system was introduced, dial phones remained completely compatible. A piece of equipment might easily be installed fifteen years after its first introduction and could have a life expectancy of twenty years, remaining in use for thirty-five or more years.

BELL'S "BUTTERSTAMP"

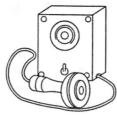

A telephone with a transceiver, a single unit for both speaking and listening. The handheld component shifts easily from mouth to ear without any need for head spinning. The piece resembles the butterstamp of the same time period used to mold butter pats.

PLACE: New Haven, Connecticut

TIME: 1878

BELL'S CENTENNIAL MODEL

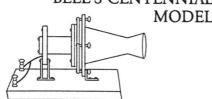

Alexander Graham Bell put together a makeshift but working model of his newly invented telephone to exhibit at the Philadelphia Centennial Exposition.

PLACE: Philadelphia, Pennsylvania

TIME: 1876

BOSTON COMMERCIAL MODEL

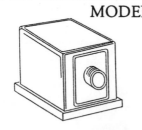

The first commercial telephone was leased to a Boston banker to communicate with his home. It had a single unit (transceiver) for both transmitting and receiving. The unit was mounted in a case resembling an early box camera. When the box sat on a table, the user had to bend over to shout into the transceiver and then spin his head to listen to any response.

PLACE: Boston, Massachusetts

TIME: 1877

"CANDLESTICK" DESK SET

A desk telephone introduced as a companion to the wall-mounted unit. The original desk set was made of brass and had a strong resemblance to a brass candle holder (with a mouthpiece mounted at its apex). As this black handheld phone evolved, it looked a lot less like a candlestick but the name stuck. The ringer was mounted in a separate box located low on a nearby wall.

PLACE: United States

TIME: 1910

COMMON BATTERY
WALL SET

Batteries used to power early telephones were located in each home. With this model wall phone the power source is located at the main switchboard and is common to all connected telephones. The handheld receiver takes a shape that remains for the next thirty-five years.

PLACE: United States

TIME: 1900

DESK SET #300

A dial telephone with a large housing to allow the bell to be installed in the base. The casing on the earliest copies of this model was made of metal. From the early 1940s to the present, the body has been made of rugged plastic. This phone is used throughout World War II.

TIME: 1937

DESK SET #500

This telephone was designed during World War II and produced immediately thereafter. In 1954 this phone was available in white, beige, green, pink, and blue. It is still used in the United States today, thirty years after being superseded by the touchtone.

TIME: 1949

DIRECT DIALING
"CANDLESTICK"

The earliest rotary dial is added to the telephone but is only practical in big cities where telephone exchanges have been installed. Most phones of this period could reach each other through a long distance operator.

TIME: 1920

"FRENCH PHONE" HANDSET
AND CRADLE

The dial was still in development but could be installed in some extensions. The bell is located in a separate box on an adjoining wall. The mouthpiece and receiver are mounted for the first time in a single handheld unit, although telephone linemen had had such a unit for work in the field since 1878.

TIME: 1928

MAGNETO WALL SET

A wall telephone consisting of a bell-ringer, a transmitting mouthpiece, and a handheld receiver. A hand-cranked magneto generator produced current to ring the operator for assistance on local calls. With this model Western Electric began to build all the hardware used by Bell Telephone.

PLACE: Eastern United States

TIME: 1882

"PRINCESS"

A bedside telephone designed for the teenager. It is compact, attractive, and comes in colors. The dial lights up and can be used as a night light.

TIME: 1956

"TOUCHTONE"

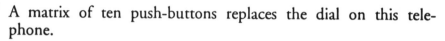

A matrix of ten push-buttons replaces the dial on this telephone.

TIME: 1964

"TRIMLINE"

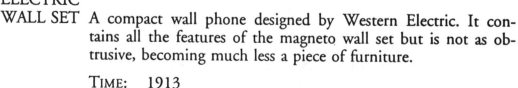

A very compact telephone the handset of which is designed to contain transmitter, receiver, touchtone buttons, and electronic ringer. An improved arrangement of twelve buttons allows the consumer of the 1980s to take advantage of extra services such as redial, speed dial, call waiting, and call forwarding. The smaller case is convenient, taking up less than half the space occupied by a standard desk set.

TIME: 1968

WESTERN ELECTRIC
WALL SET

A compact wall phone designed by Western Electric. It contains all the features of the magneto wall set but is not as obtrusive, becoming much less a piece of furniture.

TIME: 1913

Brief History of the Telephone in America

Alexander Graham Bell invents and builds the first telephone	1876
Bell refines the telephone and exhibits it in Philadelphia	1876
Box-mounted phone is available for commercial use	1877
Telephone is wall-mounted and the receiver is handheld	1882
Desk set "Candlestick" phone is introduced (and is offered for sale in the Sears Roebuck catalog)	1897
Candlestick phone is outfitted with a dial	1919
Transmitter and receiver are mounted in one handheld unit	1929
300 Desk Set is introduced	1937
500 Desk Set is introduced	1949
500 Desk Set is available in white, beige, green, pink, and blue	1954
"Princess" telephone is introduced	1956
"Touchtone" replaces the rotary dial	1964
"Trimline" telephone is introduced	1968

PART V: RELIGION

Catholic Ceremonial Objects
Jewish Ceremonial Objects

Catholic Ceremonial Objects

THE CATHOLIC CHURCH

The Catholic Church and its pattern of worship have become very stable and uniform in the western world. Any modification of the established order is met with considerable opposition. The reforms of 1960 brought greater changes in the form of worship than were seen in the previous fifteen hundred years. But with all that, the altar, the symbols, and the sacred vessels remain remarkably the same. The time period for all the objects that follow is from 300 A.D. to the present.

ALTARS

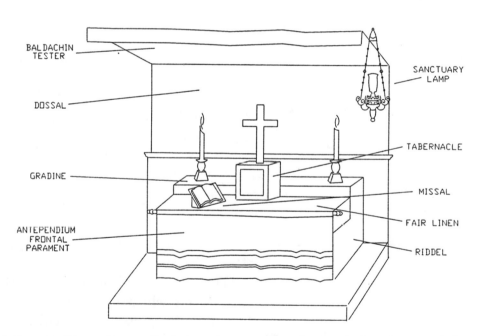

ANTEPENDIUM   A silk or linen cloth hanging on the front of the altar, pulpit, or lectern. (See Frontal.)

BALDACHIN   A metal, wood, cloth, or stone canopy over the altar.

CANDELABRA   A branched candle holder, usually accommodating an odd number of candles.

CERECLOTH   An altar cloth treated with wax to be nonabsorbent. It is exactly the size of the altar top and is the first cloth placed on the altar, lying under the fair linen.

CORONA A chandelier for the sanctuary of the Catholic church. Representing a crown, the corona is hung in place with three chains and supports seven candles.

SIZE: 4½ feet in diameter

DOSSAL A hanging of rich fabric behind an altar. It may hang in fullness or flat, either in one color or the liturgical colors, changing with the seasons of the year.

FAIR LINEN A linen cloth large enough to cover the altar and hang over each end. It covers the cerecloth and a lip hangs over the antependium. It is hemmed by hand and has a white cross embroidered in each corner.

FRONTAL An ornamental cloth covering the front of an altar. It is sometimes changed according to the liturgical season.

GRADINE A ledge or shelf at the back of an altar to receive a cross or candlestick.

LINENS The altar cloths and the linens used for communion. These include the cerecloth, protector, fair linen, corporal, pall, veil, burse, and purificator. (See individual entries listed above or under Implements of the Mass.)

MENSA A table of an altar having a receptacle for the altar stone.

PARAMENT Curtain hanging on the altar or pulpit, for example, a frontal.

RIDDEL Curtain hung at the ends of an altar.

TABERNACLE A box-like receptacle that stands in the center of the altar, containing both the bread and the wine after they have been blessed. A cloth tent covers the tabernacle when it contains the sacraments.

TESTER A flat canopy over an altar or a pulpit.

CROSSES

The major emblem of Christianity is a representation of the cross on which Christ died. The cross may have a figure of Christ affixed to it—a crucifix.

Since the death and resurrection of Christ, the cross has been used as a symbol of Christianity. Through the ages many churches have adopted a form of the cross as their own. During the Crusades certain families also incorporated the symbol of the cross into their coats of arms. The national flag of Great Britain combines the Greek Cross (Cross of Saint George) and the Cross of Saint Andrew to form the Union Jack.

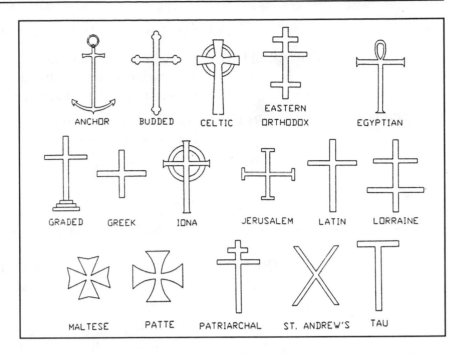

ANCHOR   The top of the anchor is shaped like a cross, symbolizing Christ as an anchor in times of distress.

BUDDED   A Latin cross with trefoil tips representing the Holy Trinity. This symbol is often found at the apex of a staff carrying the Christian flag.

CELTIC   Similar to the Latin cross but with a circle signifying eternity surrounding the center.

EASTERN ORTHODOX   The Latin cross is superimposed over the symbol for the tree of life.

EGYPTIAN   An ancient symbol, the ankh, appeared in hieroglyphics meaning "life." It was adopted by the Coptic Christians of Egypt because Christ is the "Tree of Life." Also called an *ansate cross.*

GRADED   A Latin cross with three steps at the base representing faith, hope, and charity.

GREEK   A cross having four equal arms (used by the Red Cross).

IONA   Variation of the Celtic cross.

JERUSALEM   A cross having four arms, each ending in a crossbar.

LATIN   A cross in which the upright is longer than the beam that crosses it near the top.

LORRAINE   A cross with two horizontal beams of unequal length, the wider one being near the base.

MALTESE   An eight-pointed cross formed by four arrowheads joining at their points. Used as an emblem by the medieval Knights of Malta.

PATTE   A cross having the arms narrow at the center and expanding to be wide at the ends. (Compare with the Maltese cross.)

PATRIARCHAL A cross in which the upright is twice crossed. The lower beam is proportioned similar to the Latin cross; the second beam is narrower and is placed above it.

SAINT ANDREW'S CROSS A cross having the shape of the letter "X". In heraldry this cross is known as a *saltire cross*.

TAU A cross in the form of a "T". It is also called Saint Anthony's cross.

CHRISTIAN SYMBOLS

CHI RHO A monogram made from the Greek letters XP, the abbreviation of XPICTO - Christos. These Greek letters are commonly embroidered on altar cloths.

COLORS Liturgical colors are used symbolically on the altar linens. The colors, their symbolism, and the seasons for which they are commonly used are as follows.

White Purity and joy. Christmas and Easter.

Gold An alternate for white.

Red Fire and blood. Martyrs' days and Pentecost.

Purple Penitence. Advent and Lent.

Blue An alternate to purple.

Green Hope and peace. Epiphany and the season after Pentecost.

Black Death and mourning. Good Friday.

CROWN A king's crown represents Christ as "King of Kings." A crown of thorns is a symbol of Christ's suffering.

HALO A bright disk or ring painted above or surrounding the head of a holy person as a symbol of glory.

ICHTHYS The symbol of a fish used to identify Christians in the first century. The initial letters of the Greek words meaning "Jesus Christ - Son of God - Savior" spell *ichthys*, the Greek word for fish.

IHC The first three letters of "Jesus" in Greek. It is a monogram of the name of Jesus.

INRI Latin: Iesus Nazrenus Rex Iudaeorum. Jesus of Nazareth, King of the Jews. The title written by Pilate and nailed to the top of the cross.

NIMBUS A bright cloud surrounding a deity or holy person when he appears on earth. Also the representation of this aura around the heads of holy figures in paintings.

IMPLEMENTS OF THE MASS

Magnificent cups, bowls, pitchers, and linens were produced by the early Church for ceremonial use. They were made from glass, silver, and gold.

The Mass and the objects surrounding the liturgy were pretty well set by 300 A.D. Most of the items listed below carry the same date—300 A.D. to the present.

ALMS BASIN A large plate made of wood, silver, or brass used to receive all the individual offering plates. Sometimes a velvet pad is fastened in the bottom.

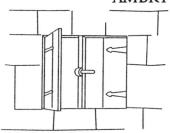

AMA A cruet used in the early Christian church as a vessel for mixing and storing wine for the Eucharist. The wine was poured from the ama into a chalice when it was required for the service. (See also Cruet.)

SIZE: 10 inches tall

AMBRY A recess in the wall of a church to store Communion vessels. The drawing shows an ambry in a 15th century church. An ambry built today will fit the architecture of the church for which it is designed.

ASPERGILLUM A brush or perforated container for sprinkling holy water.

SIZE: 9 inches long

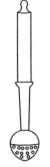

BOBECHE A small saucer placed under candles to catch the drippings. The bobeche can be made of paper, glass, or metal. The receptacle sometimes has a hole to receive the candle.

BURSE A flat, stiff envelope covered with silk, which houses the sacramental linens. The burse is used to carry the linens to and from the altar.

CENSER A covered vessel for burning incense. It is usually suspended on chains and swung in processions to spread the smoke of the burning incense.

SIZE: 12 to 15 inches tall

CHALICE A drinking cup or goblet, made of metal or ceramic, and used to prepare the wine for the Holy Communion. Wood and terra cotta cups were forbidden in the Middle Ages because of their tendency to absorb the consecrated wine.

SIZE: 6 inches tall

CHALICE VEIL A small cloth to cover the sacred vessels, the chalice and the paten.

CIBORIUM A cup with a cover for holding the consecrated wafers of the Eucharist. The covered cup is made to look like the pod of the Egyptian bean. In modern times, it is common for the ciborium, chalice, and monstrance to be designed as a set, constructed in similar style and material.

SIZE: 6 inches tall

CORPORAL A napkin-sized piece of linen cloth used in the celebration of the Eucharist. It is positioned on the fair linen of the altar and is a placemat for the bread and wine.

CRECHE A three-dimensional scene of the Nativity with the baby Christ in the manger.

CRUCIFIX A cross with the figure of Jesus crucified upon it.

CRUETS A pair of small jugs made of glass or silver, used to hold the Communion wine and the water used in cleansing the priest's fingers.

SIZE: 5 inches high

EWER A wide-mouthed pitcher used for holding and pouring water as the celebrant washes his hands. It is also the vessel used to bring water for baptism.

SIZE: 7 to 9 inches high

 FLAGON A vessel for holding wine at the Eucharist, the Lord's Supper—Holy Communion.

SIZE: 8 to 10 inches high

FONT A bowl, usually of stone, to hold the water used in a baptismal service.

 HOST BOX A container to hold a supply of wafers for Holy Communion. The box is usually round.

MISSAL A book containing all the prayers necessary for celebrating the Mass throughout the year.

 MONSTRANCE A transparent shrine in which the consecrated host is exposed for adoration. It may be displayed on the altar or carried in a church procession.

SIZE: 9 to 12 inches high

MUNDATORY A small linen napkin used to wipe the chalice and the paten. (Same as Purificator.)

PALL A chalice cover, consisting of a piece of cardboard or, more recently, aluminum, faced on both sides with linen.

PATEN A small dish, made of metal or glass, to hold the bread for the Holy Communion.

PURIFICATOR A linen to wipe the chalice and paten as Communion is administered. (Same as Mundatory.)

PYX A container in which the consecrated wafer of the Eucharist is kept. Also a small container used to carry the Host to the sick.

TIME: 1200

SACRED VESSEL Any vessel that comes in contact with the bread and wine after it has been blessed. The paten, chalice, ciborium, monstrance, and pyx are sacred vessels.

THURIBLE A container for burning incense. (See Censer.)

WAFER The disk of unleavened bread representing the body of Christ at the Holy Communion.

Jewish Ceremonial Objects

IN THE HOME

The festival celebrations and the seasons of remembering that are central to the Jewish faith were established by Moses in 1300 B.C. These rituals were passed down from generation to generation by oral tradition. They were solidified by the rabbinical schools of the 2nd century B.C., and have come to us without major alteration.

Tradition has given us no instruction to guide us concerning the form of the objects used in Jewish ritual. For instance, a designer is told that a menorah is a candlestick to accommodate seven or nine candles, the middle candle holder higher than the others, but beyond that he has total artistic freedom. A Kiddush cup must hold a serving of wine but any cup will do. It may be plain or ornate, made of any material, and with or without a stem.

CANDLESTICK A candlestick with a minimum of two candles is kept in the home for use on the Sabbath and holy days. The menorah (see Menorah) is a special candelabrum for use during Hanukkah.

ELIJAH'S CUP A wine goblet, kept in honor of the prophet Elijah and used during the Passover Seder. Every Jewish home celebrating the Seder fills this cup and puts it at a place setting reserved for this ever expected guest.

HAVDALAH OBJECTS Every Saturday night and on nights following a holy day, the head of the household recites the "Havdalah" over a cup of juice or wine and a spice box, called a *besamim*. Reference is made in the recitation to lights, so a candlestick holding at least two braided candles is required.

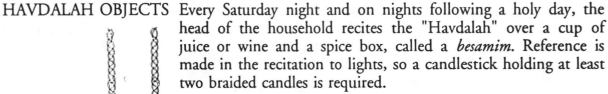

KIDDUSH CUP

The Kiddush prayer and benediction, ushering in the Sabbath and certain holy days, is recited by the head of the household over a cup of wine or loaves of bread, called *Lehem Mishneh*. The Kiddush cup is sometimes finely crafted and reserved for this celebration.

KOSHER FOOD

A food that is permitted to be eaten. A code of rules based on biblical and rabbinical ordinances forbids the consumption of certain foods. A condensation of the rules follows:

1. The flesh of an animal that has a cloven hoof and that chews the cud is allowed. Cattle, goats, sheep, and deer are permitted; horses, pigs, and camels are forbidden.

2. Birds of prey are generally forbidden; dove, quail, and poultry are permitted.

3. Reptiles are forbidden.

4. Fish that have fins and scales are permitted; shellfish are forbidden.

5. It is unlawful to consume the blood of an animal.

6. Animals must be slaughtered according to ritual and inspected for disease.

7. Mixing meat foods with dairy foods is prohibited. There are no laws concerning fruits and vegetables.

KOSHER UTENSILS

A separate set of dishes is kept for use on Passover. In kosher homes, pots and dishes used for meats are kept separate and never used for dairy foods.

MEGILLAH

A hand-written scroll containing the book of Esther. Many Jewish homes own a Megillah, and the scroll is read aloud there as well as in the synagogue.

MENORAH

A special candelabrum, traditionally designed to hold nine candles (or oil lamps) and used for celebrating the season of Hanukkah. Reform temples permit a seven-branched Menorah. The center candle, called a *Shammash*, is used to kindle the other candles.

MEZUZAH

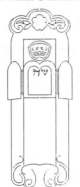

A small case, made of wood or metal, containing a strip of parchment inscribed with scripture verses from Deuteronomy. These verses direct the believer to love God and to keep his commandments. The word "Shaddai" (Almighty) is printed on the backside of the parchment and is visible when the folded strip is placed in the case. The mezuzah is commonly nailed to the outside door frame of the home and kissed before entering the house.

PHYLACTERIES A pair of leather cases to be worn during morning prayer. This is the Greek word for Tefillin (see Tefillin).

SEDER A dinner celebrating the Passover and the Exodus from Egypt. The prescribed menu includes lamb shank, a dish made of chopped nuts, apple, and cinnamon, and a green vegetable — parsley. The objects used during this observance include a pitcher and basin for washing the hands at the table, the seder plate, Elijah's cup, and a special cup for each member of the family.

SEDER PLATE A plate to hold certain items used during the Passover Seder meal: matzoh (unleavened bread) and maror (bitter herbs).

TALLIT A prayer shawl.

TEFILLIN A set of two leather cases worn during the daily morning prayer. The cases contain passages from the Torah written on strips of parchment. One tefillin cube, called *Shel Yad*, is strapped to the upper part of the left arm. The long leather strap is wrapped seven times around the arm ending in a loose knot in the palm of the hand. The other case, called *Shel Rosh* is worn on the forehead. It is tied to the skull with an easily adjusted loop. (Same as Phylacteries.)

— IN THE SYNAGOGUE —

Most of the ceremonial objects of the home are also kept for use in the synagogue. These include a Megillah, a Mezuzah on the door post, and a Menorah, available for use at Hanukkah. Occasionally the same prayers that are said in the home are repeated in the synagogue; therefore, the synagogue keeps on hand a set of the items used in the readings: a cup and wine for Kiddush, and a cup, braided candles, and spice box for Havdalah. (See In the Home.)

AMMUD   A reader's desk, placed in front of and below the ark.

ARON HA-KODESH   The Holy Ark where the Scrolls of the Torah are kept.

BIMAH   A desk placed in the center of the synagogue for the reading of the Torah.

HUPPAH   A portable canopy under which the bride and groom stand during the marriage ceremony. The huppah is symbolic of the new home the couple will build and share.

MEHITZAH   A partition separating Orthodox men and women worshippers. Conservative and Reform Jews have done away with the mehitzah, allowing the family to sit in pews and worship together.

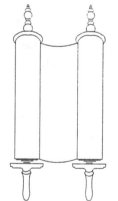

NER TAMID   A lamp that stands in every synagogue in front of the Aron ha-Kodesh. Ner Tamid means eternal light, and the lamp is never extinguished.

SEFER TORAH   A copy of the Torah, the five books of Moses, in scroll form. The text is written on leaves of parchment that have been sewn together to make the roll. The scroll is rolled on two wooden poles, each having a crowned headpiece and a finial. The scrolls are tied together with a sash and encased in an embroidered slipcase. Each synagogue must have at least one scroll, and most have several.

SIZE: 4 inch diameter; pole - 2 feet long

Sources

─── DAILY LIVING ───

Eating Giscard d'Estaing, Valerie-Anne. *World Almanac Book of Inventions.* World Almanac Publications, 1985.

Panati, Charles. *Extraordinary Origins of Everyday Things.* New York: Perennial Library, Harper and Row, 1987.

Drinking Katsigris, Costas, and Mary Porter. *Pouring for Profit.* New York: John Wiley & Sons, 1983.

Sichel, Peter, and Judy Ley. *Which Wine?* New York: Harper and Row, 1975.

Tiano, Jack. *American Bartender's School Guide to Drinks.* Nashville: Rutledge Hill Press, 1981.

Smoking Pipes Dunhill, Alfred. *The Pipe Book.* Arthur Barker Ltd., 1969.

Herment, George. *The Pipe.* New York: Simon & Schuster, 1954.

Webster, Carl. *Webster's Guide to Pipes.* Cornerstone Library, 1962.

Games and Gambling Hargrove, Catherine Perry. *A History of Playing Cards.* Mineola, NY: Dover Publications, Inc., 1966.

Scarne, John. *Scarne's Guide to Gambling.* New York: Simon & Schuster, 1986.

Sifakis, Carl. *Encyclopedia of Gambling.* New York: Facts on File, 1990.

Wykes, Alan. *The Complete Illustrated Guide to Gambling.* New York: Doubleday & Co., Inc., 1964.

Games Giscard d'Estaing, Valerie-Anne. *World Almanac Book of Inventions.* World Almanac Publications, 1985.

Furniture Aronson, Joseph. *The Encyclopedia of Furniture.* New York: Crown Publishers, 1947.

Gloag, John. *A Short Dictionary of Furniture.* Bonanza Books, 1965.

Miller, Judith, and Martin Miller. *The Antiques Directory.* Portland House, 1988.

Reif, Rita. *The Antique Collector's Guide to Styles and Prices.* Hawthorn Books, Inc., 1970.

Clocks and Watches   Milham, Willis I. *Time and Timekeepers.* New York: Macmillan, 1923.

Lamps and Lanterns   Cuffley, Peter. *Oil and Kerosene Lamps.* Victoria, Australia: Pioneer Design Studio, 1982.

Hayward, Arthur H. *Colonial Lighting.* Mineola, NY: Dover Publications, Inc., 1962.

Eyeglasses   Bronson, L.D. *Early American Specs.* The Occidental Publishing Co., 1974.

Hearing Aids   Davis, Hallowell, ed. *Hearing and Deafness.* New York: Holt, Rinehart and Winston, 1947.

Appliances   Panati, Charles. *Extraordinary Origins of Everyday Things.* New York: Perennial Library, Harper and Row, 1987.

Litshey, Earl. *The Housewares Story.* National Housewares Manufacturers Assn., 1973.

Schroeder, Joseph, Jr., ed. *Sears Roebuck Catalogue, 1908 Edition.* DBI Books, Inc., 1971.

Sears Roebuck Catalogue, 1902 Edition. New York: Crown Publishers, 1969.

Wetterau, Bruce. *The New York Public Library Book of Chronologies.* New York: Prentice Hall Press, 1990.

CIVIL AUTHORITY

Standards and Flags   Crampton, William. *The Complete Guide to Flags.* New York: Gallery Books, W.H. Smith Publishers, Inc., 1989.

Pine, L.G. *International Heraldry.* Charles E. Tuttle Company, 1970.

Punishments   Walker, Peter N. *Punishment: An Illustrated History.* David and Charles Publisher, 1972.

WARFARE

Weapons   Norman, A.V.B., and Don Pottinger. *English Weapons and Warfare.* New York: Prentice Hall, 1979.

Stone, George Cameron. *A Glossary of the Construction, Decoration and Use of Arms and Armour.* Jack Brussel, Publisher, 1961.

—— SCIENCE AND TECHNOLOGY ——

Dowsing Bartlett, Sir William, and Theodore Besterman. *The Divining Rod.* Methuen and Co., Ltd., 1926.

Vogt, Evon Z., and Ray Hyman. *Water Witching USA.* Chicago: University of Chicago Press, 1959.

Telephones Povey, A.J., and R.A.J. Earl. *Vintage Telephones of the World.* Peter Peregrinus Ltd., 1988.

"The Telephone Story." Poster. American Telephone and Telegraph.

—— RELIGION ——

Bridger, David, and Samuel Wolk. *New Jewish Encyclopedia.* West Orange, NJ: Behrman House, Inc., 1976.

Lomask, Milton, and Ray Neville. *The Way We Worship.* Farrar, Straus & Cudahy, 1961.

Gouker, Loice, and Carl Weidmann. *A Dictionary of Church Terms and Symbols.* C.R. Gibson Company, 1974.

—— GENERAL ——

Webster's Dictionary of the English Language, unabridged encyclopedic edition. Chicago: J.G. Ferguson Publishing Company, 1977.

The World Book Encyclopedia. Field Enterprises Educational Corporation.

ABOUT THE AUTHOR

Thurston James retired in 1991 after many years as Properties Master of the Department of Theater, Film, and Television at the University of California, Los Angeles. In the course of his long and illustrious career, he has built nearly every prop imaginable.

Thurston's previous books are the critically acclaimed *Theater Props Handbook, The Prop Builder's Mask-Making Handbook,* and *The Prop Builder's Molding & Casting Handbook* (all Betterway Publications).

A man of many talents, he has also been a scenic artist, shop carpenter, and lighting designer. Thurston continues to work in the theater crafts field, conducting workshops and seminars on various aspects of theater props. He lives with his wife, Rosella, in Sherman Oaks, California.

Index

INDEX TO BRIEF HISTORIES